CRYIN' OUT

CRYIN' OUT

Separation Anxiety and the Soldier's Child

Danielle Marie Batiste-Bond

With Cara Lopez Lee

To order additional copies of this book, contact:
Xlibris Corporation
1-888-795-4274
www.Xlibris.com
Orders@Xlibris.com

Dedication page:

To my son Brandon Bond who gave me the inspiration for writing this book you are my heart and soul and mommy love you dearly.

To my husband Floyd Bond my anchor, support and best friend you never stop believing and encouraging me to get this book finish you always knew I could do it and I love you for it. You are my biggest fan

To my Mom the rock who kept the family together and love us unconditionally. I wish you were here to see the finish product but I know you are saying my baby did it and I'm very proud of her. Love you and miss you dearly.

Acknowledgement page:

I would like to thank my family for believing that I could write this book and see it to the end. Thank you for all the love and support.

To my co worker Minnie Arnold you told me to go girl and you will make it no matter what, and thank you for believing in me and stood behind me all the way.

To Mark Graham and Cara Lopez Lee you two took my idea and turn it into this wonderful book that everyone can learn from and really appreciate and I really appreciate all the time and hard work spent on this book. Thank you from the bottom of my heart

ONE

When Goodbye is Confusing

My husband had been saying goodbye to our son for a month. So we thought our four-year-old was prepared. When Brandon was two, Floyd had spent a year serving in Kuwait. So we thought this would be routine. Or at least, as routine as having a husband and father absent for a year can possibly be.

When Floyd's unit was briefed for deployment to Afghanistan, the briefing included information on how to prepare children for a military parent's departure. Floyd was doing what he'd been advised to do. I left my husband and son alone together to have one-on-one time every day for several weeks, so they could talk about what was going to happen. Floyd told Brandon that he didn't want to leave us, but that it was his duty to serve our country and protect us here at home. He showed Brandon a map and said, "This is where Daddy is going to be. This is called Afghanistan." He explained the distance between Afghanistan and Virginia. He explained that the year he was gone would feel like a very long time. He told me that he asked Brandon, "Do you understand?" and that Brandon nodded.

As I pictured Brandon nodding, I imagined a sort of blankness in his

1

eyes. I realized he couldn't possibly understand. What four-year-old can understand the size of the world from looking at a map? How could my son understand the length of a year, when he couldn't understand what I meant whenever I said, "In a minute, Brandon"? Still, we did our best, and I thought that would be enough. Brandon would miss Dada. So would I. But we would be OK, just like we were OK the first time Dada left.

His father would send home videos, call as often as he could, send emails, and chat with us on Facebook. It wasn't enough for me; I don't know why I thought it would be enough for my young son. Even for an adult, the difference between being told someone you love will leave, and having that person actually go away, is like the difference between staring into a dark hole, and then leaping into it. Who knows how deep it will go, or whether you can survive the fall?

My son wasn't ready for this. That's what I know now. If only I'd known it then. "If only" would become the phrase that filled my head later, in between the screaming and the silences, the raging tantrums and the heartbreaking sobs. If only I'd had more information. If only I'd been trained in how to be the mother of a child about to be abandoned by a father who didn't want to abandon him. If only I had realized that my son's unnerving calm on the day Dada finally said goodbye was nothing more than the terrible stillness before a destructive tornado.

We were all in the gymnasium on post, families of soldiers being shipped overseas. Brandon sat in his straight back chair, fidgeting, jumping down, getting back up, muttering to another boy about his age who sat next to us with his mother, the wife of one of Floyd's buddies. She and I talked, too, but I have no idea what we said, just the typical distracted conversation of spouses and parents about to be left behind. The gym echoed with murmurs, and the occasional shout of a small child who didn't understand the solemnity of the occasion. I looked around and saw that many of the kids around us were either younger or older than Brandon, either too young to understand the idea of a parent leaving for a long time, or old enough to deal with it—though this thought wouldn't hit home until later.

The soldiers marched into the gym, and the sound of their boots on the hardwood floor reminded me of my days in the military, before I broke my ankle and received a medical discharge. I looked for my husband among the sameness of all that desert gear, and then I saw him, looking handsome in his uniform. It seemed unfair of him to look so good when I wasn't going to see him again for a year.

"Look, Brandon! There goes Dada! Dada."

He looked up at me, and then followed my finger, at first unable to pick out Dada, confused by the sea of sand-colored uniforms. Then Brandon's eyes lit up with recognition as he pointed. "Dada!" He turned to me and asked. "What they doing?"

"They're going to sing, and then the commanders are going to talk."

"Who are they?"

"The people in charge. The bosses."

Brandon seemed to accept this. Sergeant majors talked about the importance of this mission, what it meant for our country, and how proud we could be of these soldiers. At the end of the speech, the adults in the room didn't have a much clearer idea than Brandon just exactly what these soldiers were going to do in Afghanistan, only that it was a significant somehow. Brandon and his little neighbor began playing tug of war with a toy, but the game was friendly, nothing I couldn't handle so long as they wrapped this up quickly—which they did. In ten minutes the ceremony was over. Soldiers stood and inched toward the audience, as families rushed forward to hug husbands, wives, mothers, and fathers in uniform. Most of the soldiers were men, but there were women, too. The atmosphere was charged, but sad. Soon I didn't notice anyone else anymore, as I hugged my husband and we exchanged last minute reminders, things like:

"Don't forget about that bill…"

"Oh and I didn't finish that paperwork…"

"We never did call the repair guy…"

"Remember to send those videos, so Brandon can see you."

It didn't last long. I love my husband dearly, but I'm not one for sentimental scenes. I knew he had to get moving and board the bus to Langley. "Don't worry," I said. "If there's something I forget, you can call or e-mail, or we can chat on Facebook."

During the course of our relationship, we'd both been overseas at one time or another. After I left the military, I worked in a couple of jobs with military contractors, which sent me overseas to Dubai, Saudi Arabia, and Iraq. I was an independent go-getter, both overseas and at home. I'd been on my own from the time I was 18 until I was 32, and I'd been alone with my son before. I worried about my husband, but tried to push thoughts of danger or risk out of my mind. He had a job to do, and he'd be back in a year. Any other thoughts were just borrowing trouble from a future over which I had no control. But Brandon didn't have my experience on which to draw. He had no idea how to protect himself emotionally.

But he tried.

Floyd crouched down so he was on eye level with Brandon to say goodbye. "I'll miss you, buddy. I'll be back as soon as I can. I love you. You mind your mother, OK?" Brandon nodded, but said nothing. He barely glanced at his father, and when he did he looked almost bored. "OK then, bye-bye Brandon." Floyd squeezed his son in a bear hug, and I was relieved to see Brandon hug him back. Floyd's eyes filled with tears, but Brandon's eyes remained dry. I wasn't surprised. Floyd's a softy who cries at movies, family gatherings, sentimental gifts, you name it—but I'm not a crier, never have been. It's not that I'm unfeeling, I'm just not comfortable letting it all hang out. As I watched them I thought, *Brandon takes after me.* Maybe he did have some emotional defenses, after all. It seemed more like armor, and I suspected that wasn't healthy. But he was four, and the room was full of strangers. I couldn't imagine trying to force him to be more emotional: act sadder, cry, tell Dada you love him. So I just stood there.

Then Floyd stood to give me a final kiss and a hug. "Goodbye, baby. I love you."

"I love you, too," I said. Then I simply took Brandon's hand and turned away. "Come on, sweetie. It's time to go."

He accepted my hand and followed me, but turned to look back. "Daddy's not coming?"

"No, honey. Daddy has to go to Afghanistan, remember?"

As we made our way out of the gym and through the parking lot, Brandon walked slower and slower. When I strapped him into his car seat, he started whimpering. Then I heard a sniffle, and another sniffle.

"What's wrong, Brandon? You want Dada?"

He nodded.

That's when I looked up and saw Floyd walking toward the car. You see, there were a lot of family members at this event who were less stoic than I was, and they were taking a long time saying goodbye. Since few people had even begun to get on the bus, Floyd had decided to snag another chance to see us. How were we to know that this was one of the worst mistakes he could have made? We were a family, we loved each other. At that moment, I was grateful to him for coming back, for showing he loved us, for proving to his son that he'd never leave us forever. Mostly, I was grateful because I didn't know how I was going to comfort my usually stiff-upper-lip son who was sobbing in the back seat.

"Brandon's crying," I whispered.

"He seemed fine a minute ago."

"That's what I thought. But I think he was just trying to show you he could be a brave soldier like you."

At this, Floyd started crying again. "I'll talk to him."

Floyd opened the back door, and when he saw his son hiccupping with sobs, he wiped his own tears away—not wanting to upset Brandon further. Later I would think this was another mistake. We all felt sad. Why didn't we want Brandon to know? "You don't have to be afraid, Brandon. Daddy's coming back. I promise," Floyd said.

Then he left again.

Brandon cried even harder. I sat in the driver's seat and put the keys in the ignition. Then I stopped. My hands were shaking and I'd finally started crying, too. I needed to get it together. I don't know who I was crying for more: the husband I was going to miss, or the son whose father was gone.

In the coming months, I would replay that morning's sequence of events in my mind over and over: we left Daddy in the gym so he could go to Afghanistan, and Daddy promised to come back, then Brandon started crying, then Daddy came back, then Daddy left again with another promise to come back. I wonder what was going through Brandon's mind as I started the car: *If I cry again can I get Daddy to come back again? Is Daddy really leaving or is he just making it up? Does Daddy really have to go, or can he change his mind whenever he wants?*

As we drove home, Brandon buried his face in his Mickey Mouse pillow, and I didn't hear anything from him after that. He hadn't cried the first time Floyd was deployed. He was only two then. Did he remember Floyd leaving that first time? He'd always been observant and smart, and I understood that children took in more at that age than they let on. Surely he had no conscious memories of that other day, but what about subconscious memories?

That first deployment had been tough for me: a first-time mother taking care of a baby alone, trying a string of failed home businesses in an attempt to pay off debts, running a household alone, missing my new husband.

Floyd had only been back home for a year, but our life together had fallen into a comfortable routine again. He'd always loved being a dad—he had three children from a previous relationship, and he doted on Brandon. He'd never shied away from changing diapers or getting up for midnight feedings. He'd never been impatient with Brandon's crying, and never seemed to get tired of watching the same Disney movies over and over. Those two did everything together: video games, playing in the park, and reading. I'd been all but kicked out of bedtime story-time with my son. I wasn't jealous; I knew their time together was precious.

* * *

When I grew up in the small town of New Roads, Louisiana, I never had a father like Floyd. My parents were never really a couple, and though I knew who my father was, we barely even spoke until I turned eighteen. I *almost* grew up with my stepfather. Billy Ray and my mother gave me two sisters, who I adored, but he wasn't around for long. My step-dad wasn't a bad man, but he was depressed. He committed suicide when I was 12. After that we moved in with my grandmother. My uncle in Baton Rouge became the closest thing I had to father figure. Our families visited a lot. Then one day he was murdered. I still remember the last thing he said to me, "Call me if you need me."

Although I wasn't as close with my stepfather or my uncle as Brandon was with his dad, I did feel a sense of loss when they died. I suppose you might call being surrounded by so much death and abandonment devastating, but I didn't think of it that way. I don't know what I felt. Whatever feelings I had, I stuffed them away, just like Brandon did in the gym. Maybe I was afraid to show people my feelings, or maybe I was worried that if I let them out, they'd never stop.

So I was raised in a household full of women: grandma, mom, my two sisters, and me. If you imagine that being around all that estrogen made me soft, think again. Women are tough—at least, these women were. They were survivors. So I learned to survive, and I learned that I didn't need to depend on a man to take care of me. I joined the military at 18, and I started working in the civilian sector of military support services when I was 29. By the time my son was born when I was 32, I was used to overseas travel. I was so used to being Miss Independo that I didn't even marry Floyd until *after* Brandon was born. Still, I guess there were signs that I'd missed a few of my needs along the way: emotional and otherwise.

When I was in the army, I broke my ankle when I accidentally stepped into a hole during a routine morning run. The doctor didn't x-ray it, so nobody found the fracture until it had already healed wrong. I had to be discharged from the military. My ankle would never work properly again. After that, I tried to move on. I thought I had. Later, a therapist told me I suffered from chronic adjustment disorder. Apparently this adjustment problem went beyond being a little frustrated that I could no longer wear high heels or that it hurt when I danced. It seemed I didn't like losing even a little control of my life.

Then, shortly before Brandon was born, I was diagnosed with manic-depression. I could go like gangbusters on the job in Iraq, arranging travel assignments for thousands of employees. And my friends called me a hustler, in a good way, as I tried one home-marketing business after another—never letting failure stop me, just moving on to the next one. But anytime I stopped working I would fall into these random days of depression and anxiety. The doctor gave me meds and after Brandon was born I was coping better. In fact, most of the time I was fine, even when Floyd left that first time.

Later, I would find out that parents who have problems with depression and anxiety are more likely to have children who suffer anxiety disorders. But so far I'd seen no signs of trouble in my son. He was happy-go-lucky, did well in school, and came from a relatively happy, peaceful, well-adjusted family. It didn't occur to me to worry much about his mental state.

* * *

After we left the gym, my only thoughts were that I missed my husband already and that I was tired at the prospect of doing it all without him again. I'd recently enrolled in school to earn a degree in business administration. There was going to be a lot to juggle. When we arrived at home I shut off the car engine, and the juggling act began. My son still had that Mickey Mouse pillow pulled over his face, and now that the engine was silent I could hear that he was still sobbing. When I opened his door and pulled the pillow away, I was shocked; who knew one small boy could produce that much water? Both he and Mickey were soaked. I picked him up and carried him into the house.

Inside, I set him down, and we both sort of circled the den for a few minutes, like a couple of caged animals. As irrational as it may sound, I think we were both looking for Floyd. I was thinking, *right now Dada would normally be sitting right there in that chair watching ESPN, and normally we'd sit here with him.* I tried turning on the TV, but that only made the emptiness of the house more unbearable. So I turned it off and said, "Let's go upstairs." Brandon went to the computer room and started playing a game, but then he burst into tears again.

I didn't know then that Brandon's extended crying jag was a sign of separation anxiety. I only knew that he'd never cried so much in the four years of his short life.

I didn't want to be alone with this weight. I wanted Floyd to know what was happening to his son. So I got out my camera, took a picture of my crying son, and uploaded it to the computer to email to Floyd.

What I didn't do was console my son. I thought, *he has to get used to this. I have to back off and let him get his feelings out.*

Then I couldn't bear it any more, and I felt the tears coming. I didn't want to let Brandon see me cry. I wanted to be strong for my son. So I left the room, went into the bedroom I shared with Floyd, shut the door, lay on the bed, and cried alone. It may be a long time before I completely forgive myself for that. I didn't realize that it might have helped Brandon, and me, if I had stayed in the room with him and we had shared our feelings. He would have seen that it was OK to be sad, and that we would get through it together. Instead, I left my son when he needed me most. His father had just abandoned him, and now so had I—though that's not what I'd meant to do.

I didn't know it, but my son was alone.

A Note to Parents:

In the days to come, Brandon would show yet more signs of a disorder that I'd never heard of: **separation anxiety disorder.** Some separation anxiety is normal for small children: when they have to go to school for the first time, when they have to stay with a babysitter, when their parents go back to work, that sort of thing. But separation anxiety *disorder* is a much more severe, prolonged reaction. Therapists who work with military families know its more common for military kids. I can't tell you how much more common. It hasn't been studied much.

In the coming chapters, I'll share with you what happened to Brandon as our year unfolded. It was an emotionally brutal experience for both of us—and for Floyd, too, far away and unable to help. But I hope that by sharing what happened to us, and what I've learned from the experience, maybe I can spare someone else the heartbreak we endured. At the end of each chapter, I'll tell you a few things I've learned, both from therapists and from my research.

Here's one thing I've learned about preparing a child during the weeks leading up to a lengthy deployment: its easier for the child to adjust if the departing parent doesn't just explain that he or she is leaving, but if **both parents also explain in detail all the ways in which the child's daily routine is going to change.** If we had done that, Brandon might not have received as big a shock when he came home and had to sit upstairs because it was too disturbing to be downstairs without Dada. And it might have been easier to deal with all the changes to come.

One thing that can ease separation anxiety when the soldier does leave, is for him or her to **leave without too much fanfare or stalling.** Though he did it with the best of intentions, Floyd made a mistake by coming back to the car. That only confused Brandon. It also may have set him up to think there was something he could do to bring his father back, and therefore set him up for frustration when he couldn't make that happen.

One of the most important personal lessons I've learned is that, when a military parent leaves, it's important for the parent who remains behind to **acknowledge and talk about the child's feelings.** If I had it to do again, I would have sat down with Brandon and told him, in simple terms, how I was feeling, and then asked how he was feeling. We could have talked about our sadness, our loneliness, and our fears. Ultimately, I would have reminded him that we'd been through this before, even though he didn't remember, and that if we'd survived it before, we could survive it again. I knew that, but Brandon didn't. I wish I had told him.

Even though I didn't, we made it through. But it got a lot worse before it got better.

TWO

Bottled Emotions Explode

The last time I'd spent a year alone with Brandon, on Floyd's last deployment overseas, I'd prided myself on how well I handled everything on my own. It's what I'd always done: handle things. Floyd had always admired my independence and determination, and I was proud of that. I wanted to hear him say it again when he came home: "You're amazing, Danielle. I don't know how you do it." From the moment he left, I ached to share my ordinary routines with my husband, but I hung onto the image of his proud smile and homecoming hug like a good luck charm that would get me through.

At the same time, part of me resented Floyd, for leaving behind the mundane responsibilities of stateside life, for being free to play a role in something bigger than him, and for having the freedom of an independent life overseas. I'd once known that feeling, when I was working with military support services in the Middle East. I had given that excitement up for parenthood, but Floyd had not. I knew it wasn't easy for him either: stretched out on a lonely cot every night, unable to play with Brandon and watch him grow bigger and smarter by the minute, missing the comforts of family life.

I don't know how Floyd handled it, but I knew I had to keep it together for Brandon's sake, and for mine. I believed it would do me no good to give in to wishful thinking, to wallow in grief, or give vent to my resentments. So I swallowed my feelings, sucked it up, and soldiered on. Without skipping a beat, I dropped Brandon off at daycare five days a week, and showed up as usual for my administrative job at the VA Hospital.

Brandon had been going to one of the Fort Eustis daycare centers since he was an infant. He went every weekday from about 7:30 in the morning until 4:30 in the afternoon. It was a long day for a little boy, but whenever he was there he had a ball: he loved his teachers, made friends easily, and seemed to find a happy balance between play and learning. When Floyd left, at first Brandon's life, too, seemed to continue as usual. Of course it did, because mine did, and Brandon was following my lead. Unfortunately, I didn't recognize to what extent he was following my lead, or how much it might be costing him.

Every moment we spent together—whether in the daycare center at the start and end of the day, or at home mornings and evenings and weekends—Brandon followed me like a shadow, wrapping his arms around my legs, leaning his head on my arm, climbing into my lap. Sometimes Brandon seemed so attached to me that his actions mimicked mine: when I moved he moved, when I sat he sat, when I read he read. When I would go to another room, he would follow me to that other room.

If I would say that I was going downstairs to get something, he'd call down, "Mom, are you coming back up here?"

And I'd say, "Yes, I'm coming back."

Neither of us spent much time downstairs anymore, because that was the place we used to share with Dada. I couldn't bear sitting down there alone, feeling Floyd's absence all around me. And because I couldn't bear it, my son couldn't bear it. But I didn't know that.

When I took him to daycare in the morning, it took longer than usual to pry him from my leg. When I picked him up at the end of the day, he ran to me as if he hadn't seen me for a month. It made sense to me. I just figured, 'Aw, my baby loves me and he wants to be with Mommy.' I had little previous experience with children, so I had no basis for comparison. I didn't realize that he was unnaturally clingy. So in turn it never occurred to me that this clinginess might be the result of fear and anxiety: *one parent had left and failed to come back, what if the other one did, too?*

Remember, part of this clingy behavior was not only that he followed me like a shadow, but also that he copied my actions like a shadow. So when I ignored my feelings and went on with life as if those feelings didn't exist, I suppose he tried to do the same. But my emotions were still there, simmering under the surface. And so were Brandon's. I was tense and frustrated, tired and lonely—and surely Brandon could sense it. But I didn't name my emotions or talk about them, which meant he could have no way of knowing what they were. So, how could he have known to tell me about his feelings, or what they were?

Maybe I should have known that something was building up in him by that tight look on his face during the drive to daycare. His face screwed up tighter and tighter as that first month went by. But I didn't see it as a sign. Maybe because it only reflected how I felt inside, like I was winding up tighter and tighter, too. It all seemed normal. No one was talking about anything, so there was nothing to notice.

Then one day, the school called. "Mrs. Batiste, I'm sorry, but Brandon is disrupting his class and we can't get him under control. You're going to have to come pick him up."

"What do you mean? What's he doing?"

"He won't stop running around the room. At naptime he started flipping on the carpet and refused to go to his cot. He started jumping on his chair. He took off his shoes and threw them."

"I'm at work. You don't really expect me to leave for something like that, do you? I'm sorry, but I mean, how bad can it be? He's only four. Surely the teacher can handle it."

"No, Mrs. Batiste, she can't or we wouldn't have called you. I'm sorry, this is too much to describe on the phone. Really, you need to come in."

I agreed to come as soon as I could, but I was ticked at the daycare center. I figured that they were professionals and should know how to deal with something as simple as a four-year-old who was acting out. When I arrived, I found out that it was much worse than I'd thought.

"So what's going on?" I asked the head of the preschool.

She told me what the administrator had told me on the phone, but then she added. "Then Brandon started kicking and hitting the teacher."

"Oh, God," I said. Hitting a teacher was serious. Not only because it crossed a pretty big boundary, but also because it was grounds for automatic expulsion. Mostly I was worried, because, as I told her, "That doesn't sound like Brandon."

"I know. I know."

"I'm so sorry. Are you going to expel him?"

"No, no. Brandon's usually such a sweet boy, and I know his Daddy recently left. I don't think we need to report it. He's probably just having a bad day."

"Thank you so much. I'll talk to him. I'm sure it won't happen again."

"Of course. You talk to him. I'm sure he'll be back to his old self tomorrow."

So I took him home and I asked him, "What's going on with you, Brandon?"

He looked at the floor. "Nothing."

"Did you have a bad day?"

He shrugged.

"OK. Maybe you just had a bad day. But let's not let this happen again. You cannot jump up and down on the chairs, or throw things, or disobey the teacher. And most important, you can never, ever, ever hit the teacher. If this happens again, you know what's going to happen, right?"

"Yes." He knew I would pull out the belt. I had rarely done that, and I'd never done anything more than tap him with it, just a ritual to let him know that I was in charge. Just the idea of it was enough to embarrass him and make him behave. At least, it always had been before.

"So, are you going to behave for the teacher from now on?"

"Yes."

"OK then."

But it wasn't OK. That same week, the daycare center called again to say that Brandon was raging throughout the room, out of control. This time he didn't hit the teacher, but he was wrecking the room, he'd pushed one child and thrown a ball at another. I was really pissed off, again not at Brandon, but at the teachers. Brandon was still behaving fine at home, so I was certain they must be doing something wrong. I thought that if they couldn't figure out how to do their jobs, they were liable to cost me mine. I was also worried that their inability to figure out how to discipline my son properly was going to have repercussions for Brandon's development. I couldn't be with him all day, and I wanted to be able to trust the people I left him with to stand in for me while I wasn't there—not just to protect him, but to help him develop, learn, and grow.

The moment I arrived, Brandon seemed perfectly calm. I saw no evidence of the behavior they described. I thought maybe he had learned that acting out would make me come running, so I talked it over with the teacher and she agreed that he shouldn't get to go home as a reward for acting out. Instead, I stuck around in the room next door, in case I needed to remove him. But I didn't take him out of school.

"Let's let him suffer," I told the teacher. I regret that choice of words now. If only I'd realized that that's exactly what I was doing: letting my child suffer.

He didn't act out again while I was there, but he did know that I was in a nearby room. I thought my presence was keeping him in line, because he knew I would spank him if he misbehaved. It didn't occur to me that my presence might be keeping him in line *by easing his fear of being abandoned by his parents*. While I watched from the other room, he seemed so normal—smiling, playing with toys, and even sharing with the other kids. So, I went from shrugging it off as a bad day to shrugging it off as a bad week.

But soon the calls started coming in two and three times a week. "This isn't Brandon," I would say to the teachers. "This just isn't my son."

"No, it's not like him," they agreed. But they didn't know what else to say.

I was still angry with the school, but I took out my frustration on Brandon. I would drag him out of school and yell at him all the way home. The belt came out, and mostly I tapped him with it, but a couple of times I was so frustrated I hit him a little harder. "Brandon, we can't have this kind of behavior. We just can't have it!"

Sometimes I tried to talk to him. "Brandon, is something wrong?"

"I don't know."

"Why are you acting like this?"

"I don't know."

How could I expect him to know where to begin, when I hadn't shown him the way? How could he express his feelings about what was happening inside him, when I couldn't express mine? Of course he didn't know what was wrong with him, because in many ways he was mirroring the only parent he had left, and she didn't know what was wrong with her. I wasn't letting my feelings out in an appropriate way, so he didn't know how to let his out in an appropriate way. He was taking his frustrations out on school, and in turn I was unleashing my frustrations on him. So both of our feelings were finding an outlet, but neither of us was feeling any relief.

I had to pick him up from school so often that I began to skip my lunch breaks, knowing that I might have to leave work at any time. I feared being called on the carpet and possibly fired for missing too much work. I was embarrassed, tired, and frustrated. My resentment toward Floyd grew. Floyd, who didn't have to deal with any of this. Floyd who had left me holding the bag. I didn't want to admit it, but I also resented Brandon.

* * *

Sometimes I thought back to the days before I got pregnant. I'd never really wanted to have kids. I cherished my independence too much, and after witnessing the struggles of my own single, working mother, I thought motherhood seemed like a gig that could suck the life out of you. I'd taken birth control pills for years. But then I began spending so much time overseas, alone and more-or-less celibate, that I stopped taking them. If I wasn't going to be sexually active, I didn't want to deal with the side effects of the pill.

Then I started seeing Floyd. It was something I hadn't planned. We were together so rarely, and I guess after so many years of not thinking about getting pregnant, it skipped my mind that it might happen. When it did, I never considered having an abortion. I didn't believe in that sort of thing. Besides, I loved Floyd, and I didn't exactly hate the idea of having kids. I even had some rosy pictures of parenthood. I just hated the idea of giving up my independence, of being tied to a man, of being tied to a child.

When Brandon was born, I was surprised at how fiercely I loved him: how much a part of me he felt, how often I worried that something might happen to him, how certain I was that I'd do almost anything to protect him. I even liked all the little responsibilities, so long as Floyd was around to help. I loved preparing his breakfast and lunch, picking him up from school, putting him to bed—so long as I knew that Floyd would step in and take over whenever there was something else I had to do.

But now Floyd wasn't here. Now, for a year, I would never get a break from the daily grind. And on top of that, now here came the ugly side of parenthood, the part that interfered with my ability to have a life of my own: my son was an out-of-control discipline problem, and I had no idea why or what to do about it.

The teachers were at a loss, too, though it was clear they were eager to help. We all became sleuths, trying to figure out the moments or events that were triggering Brandon's outbursts, hoping to find the trail that would lead us to the source of the problem.

When I arrived at school in the morning, before he started acting out, they would quiz me: "How was he when he woke up? What did he do on your way here?"

"He was fine," I would say, almost wishing I had a different answer.

Then the answer did change. Brandon would be fine when he woke up, but the moment we got in the car he would grow quiet, his face would turn tense and worried, and he would press his lips together. I began to notice that those were the days when I was more likely to receive a call. I tried to get him to snap out of those dark moods before we arrived at school. At first I tried to be sweet, asking him what was wrong. But he still answered, "Nothing," or "I don't know." Then I tried to make him laugh, telling jokes or funny stories. He didn't smile or laugh.

On those days, when we arrived at school he would ask to go to the motor growth room. That was a room were kids were encouraged to engage in active play, and it was empty first thing in the morning. I could see by the look on his face that he was going to explode, so I would say, "Go ahead. Let it out, Brandon! Get something and throw it. Just holler." But then he'd just stand there. I'd taught him too well how to hold it all in.

I would finally give up and leave, and a few hours later the call would come. He might have learned how to hold his anger in, but he was too small to hold it in forever. He had finally exploded, turning the class upside down, scaring the other children, and upsetting the teacher.

After a month of this, the teachers and I decided it was time for expert advice. The preschool had a counselor on staff, though this was the first time I'd been made aware of her existence. She visited with me, and then Brandon. Then she came to his class to observe him. After that she called me in to talk.

"Mrs. Batiste, I know what Brandon's problem is." She ticked off a list of his behaviors, and concluded, "That's severe separation anxiety."

"What's that?" I said.

She explained that it's a normal part of childhood development for kids to act out when one or both parents leave them for a longer time than usual. She explained that it's not uncommon for military children to suffer more than other children, because parents in the service are more likely to leave for extended periods. But she admitted she'd never seen a case as severe as Brandon's.

It made me feel guilty for how harshly I'd disciplined Brandon, but I was glad to at least know the problem. Now I just wanted to solve it. I asked her what I should do. She suggested that if the problem continued I should take Brandon to a therapist. In the meantime, she said it would be a good idea if I could get Brandon to talk through his feelings about his father leaving.

That was easier said than done. When she said that, it dawned on me that Brandon never talked about his father, never even asked about him. Part of me had known all along that this wasn't completely normal, but at first I had assumed it was because he was adjusting so well. Now I realized that I'd been fooling myself.

My first attempts to get Brandon to talk were awkward, probably because I was even more uncomfortable talking about my feelings than Brandon was. But I knew it was important. So that night when he was playing a game that he and his father used to play, I took the opportunity to say, "Dada used to like to play that game. Do you remember playing that game with Dada?"

He didn't even look at me.

"Do you remember anything else Dada used to like?"

He shrugged.

I'd spent so much time avoiding this subject that he wasn't about to change the routine now. I was more than willing to do what the counselor suggested, but I had no idea how to dial this communication problem back.

That night I gave up. But I tried a different tactic a day or two later. I decided maybe it would be less threatening if Brandon and I didn't talk directly about his feelings or his behavior. We have a cat, a dog, and a fish, and I thought he might feel safer opening up if we talked about them first. So the next time he misbehaved at school, instead of scolding or spanking him, I very calmly talked about our cat, whose name is Ugly.

"Brandon, I'll bet Ugly gets mad or sad when we leave him and go to work and to school. What do you think?"

"I don't know."

"I think he does. But Ugly doesn't do bad tings when I leave him to go to work. Ugly doesn't hurt people or knock things over. Ugly behaves. What do you think Ugly does when he gets mad or sad?"

"I don't know."

I didn't know either. I realized it wasn't the best question. I decided to make an appointment with a therapist.

A Note to Parents:

In coming chapters, I'll share some tips the therapist gave me that were helpful, and also those tips that were no help at all. I'll share what I was able to change, and what problems were resistant to change because of opportunities I'd missed at the beginning. For now, let's just talk about the **warning signs** of severe separation anxiety, otherwise known as separation anxiety disorder.

The first sign I missed was that my son was clinging to me, almost sticking to me like glue. It's normal for a small child to go through that phase, but when it goes on for weeks, that can be a sign of a more severe problem. **Another strong sign: when a child regularly complains of feeling too sick to go to school or other places where he or she will be separated from you, or simply refuses to go.** My son probably had **one of the most serious signs: severe acting-out, including tantrums, aggressive behavior, and hitting.**

If I had known then what I know now, I would have looked for **severe mood changes and inappropriate emotional reactions.** In Brandon's case, these included reacting with indifference when I talked about his father, or pressing his lips together in anger when I took him to school— which he used to enjoy.

If you ask your child, "What's wrong?" and the answer is, "nothing," the child might fear you'll disapprove of the answer. **Remember,**

children suffering separation anxiety fear abandonment, so they need reassurance they won't be punished for their answers. If the answer is, "I don't know," trust me, something is probably wrong. The child is simply having trouble expressing it. In my case, when Brandon wouldn't tell me what was wrong it was likely because I'd set that example—I didn't talk about my feelings either.

If your child has separation anxiety disorder, he or she may need therapeutic help. And, remember, these problems don't exist in a vacuum—you might have some issues to work out, too.

THREE

Staying on Top of Things

If you've ever made a decision to see a therapist or to take your child to a therapist, then perhaps you know there can be a time lapse between making the decision and picking up the phone. For me, the decision to see any kind of doctor has often been delayed by self-doubt and second thoughts. I've always prided myself on being able to handle anything on my own. And I've never wanted to overreact to any situation, believing that might make things worse rather than better.

That's why I waited so long to tell everyone about the lump in my leg. When Floyd went back to Afghanistan, I decided to use some of the time I would normally have spent with him to pursue a new endeavor: trying to finally lose the weight I'd gained after my ankle injury and the birth of my son. Because of my old injury, I couldn't do strenuous exercise, so I took up walking. When I took up walking, I started to take more notice of what was going on with my legs. I'd gained weight in my legs when I was pregnant—water weight I'd thought—and the excess fat I'd put on in recent years seemed to have gone everywhere. So at first I wasn't alarmed when I saw a lump on my thigh. I touched it and it felt kind of soft and fatty, so I assumed it was fat.

I exercised more. But then the lump turned into a large knot. So I went to a doctor. He told me that I might have bumped my quadriceps and injured it, causing it to form a knot to repair itself or protect itself. But it kept growing bigger, until it looked like some bizarre science fiction alien had taken over my leg. At that point, I went to Portsmouth Naval Hospital and a doctor there said, "That's a tumor." They immediately determined that it wasn't cancerous, but I definitely had to have surgery to remove it. "If you don't it could cause serious health problems. It's in the vicinity of some major blood vessels, and if it begins to wrap around them it could create significant circulatory issues."

Without Floyd there to help me, I didn't know what I was going to do about Brandon while I recovered from surgery. I hated asking for help, but there was nothing else for it. So I asked family members to come watch Brandon while I was in the hospital. After I got out of the hospital, I asked Floyd's dad if he could help watch Brandon during my recovery. He was so eager to help out, I almost cried at his kindness.

After the surgery, I felt kind of foolish for having waited so long: they cut a ten-pound tumor from my leg. I was on bed-rest for about a month. Even after that, I was on crutches for some time.

I didn't consider keeping Brandon in daycare during that time. I didn't want him to start acting up in class at a time when I was physically unable to deal with the consequences, and I certainly didn't want to clue his grandfather in on the fact that Brandon had developed a problem I couldn't handle. I didn't want him to get the impression I was a bad mother, or that Brandon was anything less than a great kid.

So I kept my son out of daycare, and let him stay home to bond with his grandpa. The two had a wonderful time together. Brandon didn't act up very much. In fact, he was downright sweet, asking me, "Can I get you some water, Mommy?" when I was stuck in bed, or asking, "Are you OK, Mommy?" when I started hobbling around on crutches. For me, it was hard to match up the image of this thoughtful, sensitive boy, with the boy who screamed and hit and tried to tear his daycare center apart. I didn't realize that they were two sides of the same coin, that the sensitivity of Baby Jekyll was the foundation for the monster of Baby Hyde.

Then Floyd was able to get two weeks of leave to come help me during my recovery. I was tempted to tell him, "Don't come." I realized that it could just make things worse for Brandon when his father had to leave again. I worried that Brandon would start to get used to Floyd being around, just in time to feel upset by his leaving again.

Floyd spoke the same fear aloud. "Part of me doesn't want to come, because I don't want Brandon to think I'm back for good, and then go back to the same problem."

But in the end, I realized that the situation couldn't be helped. I was incapacitated and in pain, and I wanted my husband. "Yes it could make Brandon's problem worse if you come home. But you know what? I need someone here to help me. Sure, I've got other family here, but I need you, too."

So he came.

If I wasn't sure of it before, I knew instantly when Floyd returned that my son's issues really did center on Floyd's overseas service. Brandon lit up when his father was home, in a way that I'd forgotten he could. Even his grandpa couldn't get him to grin and chatter like that, and maybe most impressive, to *behave*. For fourteen days, Brandon was the happy-go-lucky, smart, funny little boy I remembered. I tried to explain to Floyd how much Brandon had changed when he was away, but the explanation sounded so trivial. Anyway, there wasn't much Floyd could do about it. He had to go back. He did try to talk to Brandon about his behavior, telling him that just because his Dada was away, that didn't make it OK to misbehave in school.

"You have to mind your mommy and your teachers. I don't want to hear that you've been misbehaving, do you understand?"

Brandon nodded, just as he had when his father had left the last time.

After we dropped Floyd off at the airport, I could see the fear and anxiety ratcheting up inside my son again. A couple of days later, we drove past the airport and he said, "Dada's there."

"No, Dada's not at the airport," I said.

"Where's Dada?"

"When we took Dada to the airport, he didn't stay there. We took him to the airport so he could get in a big plane and go back to Afbamastan." That's how my son said it, so that's how I said it: Afbamastan. I turned to look at Brandon, and saw his face fall under the weight of that information. This time I knew what that look signaled. I knew what was coming. Here we go again, I thought. When I take this boy to daycare, it's going to be hell.

Floyd's father was still staying with us, so it was a few days before I took Brandon back to daycare. But I was right. The moment he went back to school he started throwing tantrums again. It was as if his father's visit had never happened. Or at least, it was as if he hoped that misbehaving might bring his father back, if only to discipline Brandon.

Brandon probably did understand the kind of behavior his father wanted. But that didn't mean it became easier for him to obey. The problem was he didn't understand why he felt compelled to act out the way he did. His thought processes weren't complicated enough for that.

Not that he wasn't smart, or that he didn't have some inkling of what he was getting out of this behavior. Not at all. In many ways, he was manipulating his teachers and me, though it took us a while to see it, and by then much of the damage was done.

That first day back at the daycare center, it wasn't long after I dropped

Brandon off when the center's dreaded phone number showed up on my cell phone again. I was tempted to ignore it, but that wasn't really an option.

"What is it now?" I asked.

"Brandon is climbing on top of the playhouse. He's kicking and hitting other kids. When they were playing outside, he threw a toy and hit one of the kids in the forehead."

"Oh God!"

"I'm sorry but you have to come and talk to him. He's a danger to himself and the other children. This is a safety issue."

Sure enough, when I got there, I saw another child sitting out front, holding an ice pack to his forehead. They weren't exaggerating.

I was lucky my boss was understanding, and let me continue coming and going to handle my son's discipline problems at daycare. As my visits to the daycare center became more constant, I began to notice a pattern I hadn't noticed before. I sometimes witnessed other kids acting out: screaming, throwing things, and hitting. At the time, I thought they were just kids with behavior problems. As time went on, I learned that most of those other tantrum-throwing kids had parents who had left for active duty, too.

One day when I dropped Brandon off, I stopped to peer in the window as I left, just to see if he was doing OK. That's when I saw another little boy tearing up the main room. At one point, he turned to face Brandon and the other children, picked up a toy, and hurled it in their direction. Brandon ducked, and, if it weren't for the window, the toy would have hit me smack in the face. As it was, the loud "thunk!" against the glass startled me. It occurred to me that, small as these kids were, when they were out of control, they really could be dangerous.

But that's not what concerned me most at that moment. What concerned me was that Brandon was witnessing this behavior, watching this other boy's every move. A counselor came into the room to talk to the boy who was throwing the tantrum, which made sense. But I was thinking that the other teacher should have gone a step farther and removed Brandon from the scene, because she knew that he was prone to similar behavior and might be susceptible to suggestion. At the very least, she should have redirected him to another activity.

I began to wonder if Brandon had learned some of his behaviors from mimicking this other kid, or perhaps one of the other kids I sometimes noticed behaving in a similar way.

I found out that, when Brandon misbehaved, whichever teacher caught him often pushed the problem off on another teacher, who would then say, "I'm going to tell your Mommy on you," or words to that effect. I suppose they were thinking that they might get Brandon to stop acting out by frightening him with the possibility that I would come and discipline him.

They were right about the discipline. I would drag him to the car, yell at him, and spank him. As the behavior grew worse, I tried to take things away from him, too. He loved his Play Station and his cartoons. So I often took away those things. But he soon learned to get around those punishments. I couldn't stand watch over him every minute, so when I left the room he would do things like sneak into another room and turn the TV down low so I couldn't hear. I once caught him turning it off as I walked in.

"You had that TV on, didn't you?" I said.

"No."

"Brandon, I saw it. That TV was on. I told you not to turn it on."

He said nothing, just walked back to his room and got under the covers, acting like nothing had happened.

"OK, I'm learning you," I said. "Don't think you can get away with that again. No TV."

My point is: if separation anxiety was his issue, then he was ultimately getting the results he wanted from his bad behavior at daycare. He had learned that if he flew into a violent rage, the teachers would call me and I would come get him. So what if he got a spanking? That only lasted a moment, and it wasn't what scared him most. *What scared him most was being abandoned by his parents.* So what if he got his privileges taken away? He could either sneak around me, or he could get used to not having whatever it was. He had figured out how to make me come whenever he wanted, and that was a power he couldn't resist. Did he consciously think of it that way? Maybe, maybe not. But he was definitely manipulating me, manipulating all of us.

I have to give him credit. He had a problem, and he'd figured out a solution. It just wasn't a functional solution. Of course, it took me a while to put all these bits of information together into the cohesive picture I'm presenting to you know. At first, I didn't see the patterns. I only knew that something had to change.

I had tried talking with my son about his feelings over his father's absence, but Brandon didn't want to talk about that. I had tried disciplining him, but that didn't change anything. When the teachers and I realized that he was manipulating us to get me to come pick him up, I tried to stop showing up every time he misbehaved. But that didn't work either, because he always escalated it to such a dangerous point that they had no choice but to call me. We were too late with this solution; he'd learned the system too well. Sometimes he didn't wait for them to say, "I'm going to tell your Mommy." Sometimes he said it himself, "I know. You're going to call my Mommy." That was exactly what he wanted.

In fact, one day I dropped him off at 8:00 and by 8:05, when I was still downstairs sitting in the parking lot, they were already calling me. This time, Brandon hadn't started freaking out yet, but all the other kids were eating breakfast in one area of the room, and Brandon was standing alone on the other side of the room, refusing to participate. He knew there was a rule that he had to participate or he wouldn't be allowed to stay. I walked in, prepared to reprimand him and make him stay. But he gave me that look, that tight-faced look that said without words, "If you don't take me home now, I'm going to tear this whole place apart." By this point, I realized what was happening. But I didn't know what to do. If I left him, he would run through the place like a hurricane. I felt I had no choice. I took him home.

I was still upset with the daycare providers. They were supposed to be experts in childcare, and they worked at a military base, so it seemed to me that they should know about separation anxiety. I talked it over with them, saying that I knew they must have other kids in the center suffering from the same problem as Brandon. Heck, I'd witnessed it. So, I said, they must have some ideas about what to do, or at least have come across parents who had found solutions. But they shook their heads. They had talked with other parents. *"No knows what to do with these kids," one teacher told me.*

"This is ridiculous. If this is a problem with military kids, and you have a daycare on a military base, it seems as if someone ought to know what to do, or how to handle it."

The answer was more or less, "I'm sorry, Ms. Batiste. This kind of emotional problem just isn't our area of expertise."

With that, I began looking for another daycare center, hoping to find a place that was more capable of handling this type of behavior. I also remembered my earlier plan: that if Brandon's out-of-control behavior continued, I would take him to a therapist. I first took him to his primary care doctor. I told the doctor that a counselor at Brandon's daycare said he was suffering severe separation anxiety, and I asked for a referral to a good therapist. He gave me a referral for a therapist I'll call *Dr. Smith*.

Dr. Smith had a session with me first, so that I could tell her what

Brandon was going through. Now that I think about it, she probably also wanted to talk to me first so that she could determine what *I* was going through. It had somehow escaped my notice that my own emotional state was one of the driving forces behind Brandon's. But as a children's therapist, surely she must have known to explore my life for clues to Brandon's problems. I'm not sure what she figured out about my issues in just one visit. She said that she next wanted to meet with Brandon alone.

But when I brought Brandon for his first visit, he absolutely refused to go into Dr. Smith's office without me. Then, when I tried to leave, he refused to stay. The only way I could get him to stay for the session was if I stayed in the room with them. I suppose this made sense—after all, he was suffering from separation anxiety disorder. I'm not sure it was very productive though, because she was unable to observe how he behaved when I wasn't around, and his behavior when I wasn't around was the problem that had brought us there.

Still, Dr. Smith did get quite a dose of the pill he could be. Here was a stranger who was trying to get him to tell her what was going on with him, when he didn't even want to tell me, or his favorite teachers, or anyone else. Every time she tried to engage him in conversation, he made a point of ignoring her. He looked around the room as if she wasn't there, looking at and touching things, and refusing to make eye contact or any verbal response. When we got him to sit in the chair, he fidgeted and rocked and tapped his feet and hands, unable to sit still.

Finally, she and I had a conversation, but it was stilted and awkward. I guess I shouldn't have been surprised that Brandon took no interest in talking to her, because I didn't want to talk to her, either. There was something clinical and aloof about her, with no warmth or friendliness to offset it. I felt that my son and I were two equations she was trying to solve. If Brandon was mirroring my emotional state, then we needed to find a counselor who I could trust, so that he would trust that person, too.

That's all hindsight. At the moment, all I knew was that this woman had come recommended by my son's doctor, who I did trust. She told us to come back in two weeks. So we did. When we came back, I immediately knew that the two-week interim between sessions was a mistake, because when I told Brandon, "We're going back to see Dr. Smith," he asked, "Why?"

"So we can help you solve your problem at school. You remember Dr. Smith, don't you?"

"No," he said.

I don't know if that was true or not, but when we arrived it certainly seemed as if we were starting all over again. Neither of them had gotten anywhere in the first session, and he went through the same series of behaviors again: avoiding her eyes, not responding to questions, shaking and rocking and wandering the room. Unable to shake her off, he finally escaped through the only tactic left to him: he fell asleep. I asked her if we could schedule sooner than two weeks, but she suggested we keep that schedule and decide what to do from there.

The next time I brought him to her, I don't know how much he remembered, but he recalled enough that when we pulled up to the building, he said, "I don't want to go in there." Why should it be any different from daycare? He didn't want to go there either.

This time she tried talking to him alone again. She pulled out a board game, Candyland. He played with her, and to do that he wasn't able to completely ignore her. They took turns, and he moved his piece around the board. He also stopped running around the room. But he still refused to look at her or talk to her. I thought, "This is going nowhere." I thought maybe if she would see him at least once a week, instead of every two weeks, this might work. Two weeks might as well be an eternity for a four-year-old. How could they bond if they only saw each other for one hour twice a month? He clearly hated being there, and I hated it, too. Nothing was happening. He seemed determined to ignore her for as long as it took to get rid of her, just as he was determined to tear up his daycare for as long as it took—for his Daddy to return, or for me to show up, I suppose. I decided this was pointless, and I didn't take him back to therapy.

I realize now that perhaps three visits weren't enough to tell me whether or not he could make progress with her. Maybe the Candyland game was the first sign of the ice cracking, and he might have thawed out in a few more visits. Maybe I should have insisted on more frequent visits until she agree. Probably I should have tried another therapist that I felt more comfortable with, or at least one Brandon felt more comfortable with. The relationship between a therapist and a patient is very intimate, so finding the right fit is important. I have to admit that I was impatient, because not only were those six weeks with that therapist long for a four-year-old, they were interminable for me—as Brandon's behavior at the daycare center continued out of control.

I did seriously consider taking him to another therapist. But then, for no reason I could figure, a sudden calm descended on Brandon. For a few weeks, he seemed better. I felt confident it wasn't because of the therapy, because the change came after we stopped the therapy. Later, it would occur to me that maybe he'd simply worn himself out, or had given up and fallen into a depression.

Or maybe he was quietly recharging his batteries for another round.

A Note to Parents:

Each mistake I made along the way compounded the problem that

Brandon had in dealing with separation anxiety. So, as time went on, we had much more to solve than we would have if we'd addressed the potential problem from the moment we knew Floyd would be deployed. I see now that it wasn't enough for Floyd to explain that he was leaving, or even just to tell Brandon the ways in which his life would change. **We really should have offered him some coping strategies *before* things changed.**

I realize now that I could have done a few simple reassuring things that might have helped us avoid his initial outbursts at school. The first, and most important would have been to **talk about our feelings** the day Floyd left. I could have given Brandon a signal that it's healthier to talk about our fears rather than act them out. Talking about my feelings might also have given me some relief, so that Brandon would not have picked up on *my* anxieties.

When he went back to school, he was not only missing his father, but must certainly have been afraid I would be next. Experts on separation anxiety say that it can be helpful to **reassure a child that you will return, and to remind him that he survived the last separation. Simple, repeated goodbye rituals can help with that reassurance.** So, Brand and I could have come up with a daily sign between us that served as my reminder that he could count on me to be back at a certain time each day. This could have been as simple as a secret handshake, hand signal, or last wave through the window, even a fun exchange like "See ya later, alligator… after a while, crocodile." **Following predictable and consistent patterns throughout each day is another important way to instill confidence in a child and reduce anxiety**

Child psychology experts say **its important not to give in to manipulations.** Of course, Brandon's more violent outbursts made it nearly impossible for me *not* to give in and come get him: once he became a danger to himself and others, there was no way the daycare would have said, "Stay away, because we know if you give in now we won't be able to control him in future." They needed to solve their immediate problem. However, there were moments early-on when we might have used other measures: such as me **promising to call him once a day** so long as he behaved, or me **promising him special time together** so long as he behaved.

Perhaps the daycare workers could have created a time-out room, rather than calling me at the first sign of trouble. After all, they too have a vested interest in not reinforcing the children in their care to repeat these behaviors.

As for counseling: therapy isn't an instant cure, and not every therapist and patient are going to be a perfect fit. I see now that I could have given Brandon's relationship with his therapist more time to work, or been more assertive about requesting more frequent visits, or at least followed through with trying another therapist. I also think some of Brandon's problems might have been avoided if I had seen a therapist early on to deal with my own anxieties.

Children can be very sensitive to their parents' emotional issues. Self-awareness is called for here. If you have a child and your spouse is going off to war, counseling can be a proactive way to deal with reactions of grief, fear, and stress that are normal for anyone in that situation. In this case I'm talking about counseling for you, the parent. You might find that you don't need it, but hey, what do you have to lose if you try it? More important, consider what your family potentially has to lose if you don't.

FOUR

It Takes A Village to Screw Up a Child

You're likely familiar with the saying, "It takes a village to raise a child." I believe it works the other way, too: it takes a village to screw up a child. Often it starts with the best of intentions. Luckily, good intentions also help us to recognize when our efforts aren't working, so we can change course. I just wish more of the people in Brandon's life had been better informed about separation anxiety disorder from the beginning, so we wouldn't have found ourselves changing course so many times.

The bottom line is that Brandon has been lucky to have so many people care about him, because love has the power to overcome many mistakes. Ultimately, my son will likely be fine. But looking back, now I can see several ways in which we all accidentally contributed to the scars he picked up along the way—many of them the results of our efforts to set things right.

As I've said, I did try talking to Brandon when I saw that he was struggling. But it was hard to give up on my previous solutions, until I saw that these talks were starting to work. Unable to convince Brandon to discuss his feelings, I wasn't immediately ready to let go of the idea that corporal punishment might set him straight. On top of that, as his behavior escalated, so did my stress, and so did my willingness to literally whip him into shape. I can see now that, in many ways, I was terrified. I feared that my child was turning into someone else entirely, possibly someone mentally ill, or maybe even possessed.

I'm ashamed to admit it, but my inability to cope with his behavior, and the inability of people I'd expected to be experts to do any better, all made me desperate enough to grasp at any straw. And one of those straws was demonic possession. This strange idea didn't come to me just because he threw tantrums or hit people. The most disturbing thing for me was the way he seemed to become someone else, or something else, whenever he lost control. His face was so altered, it seemed that the Brandon I knew vanished.

One of the times Brandon started hitting and kicking the other kids, the daycare staff called to tell me they'd taken him outside to blow off steam. It didn't work. He'd thrown off his shoes and was alternately kicking the door with his bare feet or climbing up the door and banging on the window. They feared he might break a toe, injure his hand, or fall from a high spot on the doorframe and hit his head. He never let up during my long drive to pick him up. When I arrived I could hear him still hurling himself at the door and kicking it.

When I was finally able to crack open the door without fear of hitting him, I stepped outside, took one look at my son, and received a cruel shock. His face was set in a grimace of rage that made him look deranged. His eyes looked as if he were somewhere else, and something evil had taken his place. I couldn't help the idea that popped into my head: I thought he looked like a demon. At that moment it was an abstract thought, not literal.

I calmly told him to stop. I tried to pull him away from the door, but he fought me off, hitting, kicking, and spitting. I shouted at him. But he just kept going. Then I stepped aside to talk with the two members of the staff who were overseeing the situation.

"He's been doing this for at least twenty minutes now," the center's counselor said. "I've never seen a tantrum last this long."

"What's going on? Is he frustrated?"

"We don't know. This is the worst we've seen him."

It wasn't the first time they'd tried to solve the problem by taking him outside. It was a solution the teachers and I had reached together. Sometimes when he started spiraling into a rage, they would take him outside and let him run up and down the hill behind the center, or throw a ball until he wore himself out. It often worked. He got it out of his system, or simply wore himself out, and then he would calm down. Looking back on this particular day, I guess he'd finally wised up and figured out what we were doing. Likely, he wanted to regain his control of the situation by upping the ante. Remember, my son was afraid of separation; that's why control was so important to him.

"OK, now what?" I said. "What else should we try?"

They shook their heads. None of us knew.

I suppose Brandon wanted to go home. But even though he knew that I had to take him home after an outburst like that, he still didn't stop right away. I'm guessing that's because he was stuck between a rock and a hard place. He knew that if he threw a tantrum I'd come back, and he knew that if the tantrum were big enough I'd have to take him home. But he also knew that, once we left the daycare center, he was in for a whipping. So when I said, "Let's go to the car, now!" he would just thrash around some more.

He finally did wear himself down, and we left. Then when we got to the car, I spanked his little behind, hard. I got into his face yet again, screaming my frustration. "What is going on with you? Why do you kick people? Did you know you could hurt someone?" It didn't occur to me that I was asking for reasons from a child too young to understand his own motives for doing anything. "Did you know you could hurt yourself kicking that door?" Of course he didn't know that. "What's gotten into you?" I didn't expect an answer to that one.

It scared me when he answered, "He told me to do it." At the moment it didn't occur to me that I might have put the idea in his head, by mentioning the idea of something getting into him.

"*He?* He who?"

"He's the one who tells me to kick people. He told me to kick the door."

"One of the other kids told you to do it?"

"No."

I'm a logical person. I didn't really want to think that some evil being might be telling my son what to do. So I tried to get the conversation back to normal, and said the only thing I could think of: "Look Brandon, I was there. There was no one else there. Anyway, no matter who tells you to do something, if you know it's wrong you don't listen to them. You listen to me. You don't listen to nobody else but me. You understand?"

"Yes."

But the next time he was caught hitting or kicking or spitting, he used the same excuse, "He told me to do it."

Those words were still in my head the time after that, when I showed up yet again to witness him going berserk. I stared, dumbfounded as he tore the motor growth room apart, picking up every single toy and chair and throwing or heaving it. Nervous teachers shepherded the rest of the bewildered children out of the room. A couple of teachers tried to calm him down, in soft, sweet voices, "Come on Brandon. Stop it now. Calm down, baby." It was baby talk, like he was two instead of four. I didn't question that approach at the time. I just studied his face, trying to find some sign of my son. But he was gone, replaced by something wild and inhuman, apparently unaware of the people around him. While he raged on with no signs of stopping, one of his teachers, a devout Christian woman, pulled me aside to talk privately.

She said that it seemed as if my son might be possessed by something evil. "Do you see the way his face is all twisted? That's not the sweet Brandon we know. It's like he goes off to another realm, and some other spirit enters him. You've got to get that spirit out of there."

After an hour of violent rage, he finally came back. That's what I call it: he came back. When he was finished, the room looked like a scene from a movie in which some dangerous underground organization tears someone's home apart to find a secret file.

By that point Brandon had been struggling with severe separation anxiety for months, and I was exhausted. So I was pretty suggestible, and, though at first I hadn't thought of the word "possessed" in literal terms, now that his teacher had spoken it aloud I seized on it. Please understand, although I believe in God, I'm not typically a churchgoer, and I'm not usually superstitious. I don't think I would have grabbed onto the idea, except for the faint hope that this might be a problem we could actually solve. I'd already tried everything to deal with his emotional problem, with no success. I had yet to try solving it as a spiritual problem.

No, I didn't seek an exorcist. But we did start going to church. I started praying. We'd stand there singing in church, and I'd stare at my son, who looked as bored and antsy as any four-year-old might, and I'd think, "I'm going to get this thing out of you." I realize now that these were crazy thoughts. But I was alone with this unending problem, missing work, missing sleep, missing my husband—and I guess I was coming a little unglued.

Church did help me. God did help me. A spiritual approach did help me. As I started praying, I started to feel calmer. But though it helped me, it didn't help Brandon, at least not directly or quickly.

The calls from the daycare center kept coming with increasing frequency, until I had to return to the center every day. Sometimes I could go there and talk to him and come back to work. Other times the day was shot. His daycare was a 20-minute drive from work, and during the whole drive my mind was spinning: "I can't take this, I can't take this, I can't take this! I'm burning up gas. I'm tired of going to this daycare center. I'm going to lose my job."

Luckily, that last item was up to me; I had told my boss exactly what was happening, and he'd asked me not to quit, told me to take the time I needed to handle this problem. He'd said that family comes first, that he knew I was doing the best I could, and that the problem couldn't last forever. But I wondered about that. I felt guilty, leaving work all the time. I realize now that this is what community is about, that not everyone in the village who helps raise a child works directly with or for that child—sometimes they just make it easier for the rest of us to do what we need to do. I was grateful to my boss and my coworkers.

However, I was much less than grateful to those daycare workers. Each time I came to deal with him, I made little effort to disguise my eye-rolling disdain and frustration. "Y'all can't handle a four-year-old? Come on! You're supposed to be child care experts." I still get a little irritated when I think that some of the staff may not have been as well trained as I expected. But I also realize that a lot of my emotional reaction was really guilt, because I was his mother and I couldn't handle him either.

While his rages seemed to tower larger than life, he also began to show us the flip side of his problem, which was almost more alarming. In between explosions, he resorted to exaggerated babyish behavior. He didn't just act like a baby—he acted like an infant. Sometimes, without being told, he'd sit or stand in a corner, and then he'd just stare blankly into space. As time went on, he began doing that while sticking two or three fingers in his mouth. *Sometimes he rocked, as if he were autistic.*

This combination of behaviors worried the center's counselor, who said, "He seems to be regressing to an eleven-month-old."

That made me angry. I thought she was saying he was immature or mentally disabled. "What do you mean?"

"It's not a put-down. I'm just saying he acts traumatized."

"OK. But what should I do?"

"Talk to him."

I knew she meant for me to talk with him about his feelings, which I'd already tried with no success. Giving up was not an option, so I racked my brain for a new tactic. I decided to try to get the conversation started by addressing the hand-sucking first, trying to convince him to stop. Brandon is a little bit of a germ freak, a Mr. Clean; he gets that from me. So whenever I saw him put his hands in his mouth, I said things like, "Brandon, you know how you don't like germs? Your hands are germy. And when you put them in your mouth you can get sick," or "Yuck, you're making your face goopy. Don't put your hand in your mouth. That's nasty." But he kept doing it, as if I hadn't said anything. I think he would have stopped if he could have. But it was a compulsion, a way of comforting himself through what he was experiencing as his father's abandonment, and through his fear that I would abandon him next.

By August, these two problems had spiraled until, somewhere between the rages and the infantile withdrawal, I worried that my son was just plain going to lose his mind. That's when the daycare center called me and said, "Brandon slapped and scratched a teacher."

"I'm on my way," I said.

When I arrived, the director called me straight into her office. I felt as if I were the one in trouble—called into the "principal's" office for bad parenting. "I'm sorry, Ms. Batiste," the director said. "We can't have this kind of dangerous behavior in our school. This time we have to suspend Brandon. He can't come back for two days."

"OK, fine. But can you please tell me what's going on? I know everyone keeps talking about separation anxiety. But this is just over the top. Brandon loves Ms. Julie. I can't believe he'd hit her. Can you tell me exactly what happened?"

"All I know is that he slapped a teacher and scratched her. You'll have to ask her if you want to know more. Whatever happened, we have to suspend him. That's our policy. We've already let this go too far." No kidding, I thought.

I left the office, walked out to Brandon sitting on a tiny chair in the hall, and told him, "Come on! You're going to apologize to Ms. Julie."

"But I didn't do anything!"

"Don't give me that. I don't want to hear anything from you until after you apologize to Ms. Julie."

We walked into the classroom, where he dragged his feet as I propelled him over to the teacher. He stared at the ground and said, "I'm sorry, Ms. Julie."

She gave us both an odd look, but at the time I assumed it was because she was nervous or embarrassed about him coming back into the room after he hit her. Then, as Brandon and I were walking to the parking lot, the director chased us down.

Out of breath, she said, "It wasn't him."

"What the hell are you talking about?" I asked.

"Brandon didn't do it."

"So, y'all called me from my damn job and told me to come up here because Brandon slapped the teacher and scratched the teacher, and Brandon did this and that, and he didn't do it?"

She said, "I'm sorry, but that's right. Julie came to ask me why you had Brandon apologize, because it wasn't him. The teachers were trying to figure out why you were even here."

"I'm here because y'all called me."

"I know, and I apologize. Anyway, someone did hit Ms. Julie, but it was another kid. When I walked into the room, there was still a lot of confusion. Brandon was sitting right there, so I took him to the office."

"So you just assumed it was him?"

"I *am* sorry, but certainly you can understand…"

"Because it's *always* Brandon?"

She couldn't deny it. She could only tell me that Brandon would not be suspended after all, of course. Meanwhile, I stepped up my search for another daycare.

As frustrated as I was at the inability of the daycare providers to control a small boy, the staff had done one thing I couldn't have done on my own. Their counselor had identified his separation anxiety, the teachers continued to verify it, and so did Brandon. In between the screaming and throwing and spitting, when the teachers asked him what was wrong, Brandon would say just one word: "Dada."

I told the school counselor that therapy hadn't worked for Brandon. She didn't criticize me for not giving it more of a chance. She simply suggested that I continue to meet with a family therapist on my own, in hopes of coming up with some parenting solutions. So I sat with a therapist over and again, and we brainstormed on ways to alleviate Brandon's anxiety.

One solution: I pasted a photo of his dad in his cubby and suggested to Brandon that whenever he started to feel angry and out of control he should look at his dad. That didn't work. It might even have been counterproductive. This was a tried-and-true method for separation anxiety in children whose parents were still in their daily lives. The photos served to remind them that their parents would still be there for them at the end of the day. But Brandon's father had been gone an interminable amount of time, as a four-year-old senses time—heck, even as I sensed time—and he would continue to be gone for an interminable amount of time to come. So here was Brandon, regularly ready to blow a fuse because his father was gone, and to calm him down, I was asking him to stare at a photo of the one person he wanted most and couldn't have. It made no sense.

The counselor also came up with breathing techniques that I could share with my son. "If you feel the anger coming, just stop and take slow, deep breaths until you feel better." I showed him how. That didn't work either. His breathing just kept coming harder and faster until he exploded, the same as always.

My mother told me that part of the problem was that I was still spanking Brandon regularly. She said all I was doing was winding him up tighter, making him more frustrated and frightened. I couldn't disagree. It seemed that the more I spanked him, the more he tried to toughen up and act hard, like nothing bothered him. That was certainly counterproductive, because bottling up his emotions was part of what was making him so volatile.

"Talk to him," my mother said, over and again. So I did. But this time, instead of just adding talk to the equation, I also subtracted the spanking and shouting.

One reason I was finally able to approach him that way was because I was getting my own feelings under control. I was using the breathing techniques I'd learned from the therapist. I was using the power of prayer that I'd learned in church. I was taking the expert advice I'd read on separation anxiety that suggested I had to get my own anxiety under control if I expected to have any affect on my son. I began to notice that, whenever he misbehaved, if I spoke calmly and rationally, although he didn't exactly stop instantly, he did stop sooner. That was a start.

Then the center switched him to Room 119, where there were older kids and a new teacher. Brandon began to behave. For the first time it seemed as if things might get better long term. For one fleeting moment. But we were only in the calm eye of the storm.

A Note to Parents:

Although I'd tried to encourage my child to talk about his emotions, by combining that approach with physical punishment I'd probably made him feel unsafe to talk. This may have contributed to Brandon feeling emotionally alienated. Giving consequences and standing firm can help, but I discovered that **spanking is counterproductive, at least when it comes to separation anxiety.**

Talking to my son, minus the hitting, was a start. But there was still a piece missing. Brandon was too young to know how to talk about his feelings. Once you have a clear picture that separation anxiety is what's bothering a young child, **you can't exactly expect the child to start the conversation.** When you discuss these things, **it makes sense for you to be the one who names the feelings he or she might be experiencing.** Even if you're not an expert, you *are* the grownup, and that makes you better equipped than your child for understanding emotions.

Because parents and children can feed one another's anxieties, one thing that made Brandon more responsive to my later attempts at conversation was that I had started to work on getting my own anxieties under control. **If your child suffers from anxiety, getting help for your own anxieties can often be a critical component to relieving the problem.**

Although the daycare center's counselor recognized the symptoms of separation anxiety, **it would have helped if the entire daycare staff were trained to identify early warning signs.** Then I might have been able to try prevention strategies before things spiraled out of control. **It would**

have helped if the daycare center had handed out literature or offered a talk on the subject early on. By the time I was informed, Brandon's negative coping strategies had become entrenched.

One simple, concrete way I might have helped prevent some of Brandon's anxieties could have been by spending a brief time interacting with him at his preschool at the beginning and end of each day. That way he might not have felt so much of a distinction between his life with me and his life at daycare. **Experts in separation anxiety suggest that parents identify a child's interests, involve them in those interests the moment they arrive at school, and engage in side-by-side play.** At the end of the day, it's important not only to talk about what the child did wrong at daycare, but also to **offer praise for the things the child has done well.** In short, it's important that your children understand that you trust in the safety of the environment where you're leaving them, that you will return, and that when you come back they will be safe with you again.

Looking back, I regret my us-versus-them thinking. Instead of merely reacting to the younger staff's lack of expertise, I wish I'd been pro-active about requesting mutually approved strategies and insisting that the entire staff stick to them. Instead, I caught different teachers treating Brandon differently: some were assertive, others babied him, and yet others simply called me the moment things went wrong. When we did come up with mutual solutions, we were all so fed up that we often gave up too quickly, robbing Brandon of consistency.

Communication, consistency, community. Those were the keys to addressing my son's problem.

FIVE
Waiting for Results

One day the daycare center called me to tell me that I had to come deal with Brandon because he wouldn't stop making noise. When I arrived, it was naptime and all the kids were lying on cots sleeping, except for Brandon. He was lying on his cot, all right, but he wasn't sleeping. He was looking around, rocking back and forth, and making a repetitive humming noise, "Ummm-hummm, ummm-hummm, ummm-hummm…."

Concerned by his odd behavior, I turned to a teacher and said, "What's he doing that for?"

"He's been doing that for a while now, because he doesn't want to go to sleep."

I probably wasn't very good at hiding the condescension in my voice. "OK, so if he doesn't want to go to sleep, why don't y'all just have him do something else?"

"We can't make exceptions, or we can't maintain discipline. This is naptime, so everyone has to nap."

"Right, except he's not napping. If the idea is to have quiet time, and he can't sleep, I'm sure he can do a quiet activity like sit and draw, or practice spelling his name, or read a book. He loves to read." I pointed out that it couldn't be good for class discipline to have one kid lying there rocking and making weird noises."

But she was adamant about how important his routine was.

"Oh, come on!" I bit my tongue before I went on to say that it didn't seem like routine was so important to them all those times they called me to come get him. There wasn't much insistence on maintaining routine in that. I think their strict adherence to rules that I thought could be bent without being broken, while at other times not bothering to enforce rules and letting this or that kid run riot and tear up the class made for an incoherent system of discipline.

It was now several months into Floyd's tour in Afghanistan, and there was only one thing I knew for sure: if my son was going to have any luck getting over his separation anxiety, he needed boundaries more than ever. Giving him loving reassurance that I would be there for him wasn't enough. He also needed reassurance that the world would operate in some consistent, predictable manner. But since he was going through a crisis, that predictability also needed to include flexibility. These teachers seemed to have neither.

I'd finally given up on the idea of taking him to another daycare facility. His father's military benefits helped pay for this one, which was on-post. In any case, I was concerned that it might even be more disruptive to his need for stability if I changed his school. Certainly some of his teachers were great with him, and I didn't want to take him away from them, especially because when he was in the care of those particular teachers he seemed to make progress with his emotional distress. If only he could have been in their care 100 percent of the time.

Part of me understood that this problem of connecting or not connecting with teachers would be something Brandon and I would have to face throughout his childhood, as he went from school to school. Not all teachers were going to be the right fit, and I couldn't always reshape the world to fit my son. I didn't want to make things worse by acting as if every time he had a problem, we could just yank him out of one situation and put him in another. And sometimes it simply seemed as if the devil I did know might be better than the one I didn't.

By fall, Brandon had started spending part of his day at a preschool, which was at a completely different location, and some of the kids there seemed to have even worse problems than those at the daycare center. So if I moved him, who was to say it wouldn't be even worse elsewhere? I did visit a couple of possibilities early on, but when I explained Brandon's severe separation anxiety they all seemed equally at a loss to explain what they might do to help him. It's not as if there were a daycare center specially designed to deal with kids suffering separation anxiety disorder as a result of military deployment (though maybe there should have been).

For the moment, my kid refused to sleep, or to stop humming, and there wasn't much I could do about it on the spot. So I took him home, and missed the rest of the day's work.

Not that I can pin all the blame on Brandon's teachers. There's plenty of that to go around for all of us. It's not as if it's easy disciplining a four-year-old, and it's even harder when you realize that their misbehavior is sparked by fear and anxiety in the first place. I certainly didn't want to make Brandon's fears of abandonment and separation even worse. As the only parent who was still there for him, I also didn't want to become the one parent he feared most.

Spanking sometimes seemed like an easy solution, because it was such a quick, uncomplicated form of communication. But I'd already seen that, for Brandon, this increased the trust issues between us, and increased his acting out. It became too easy to use hitting to take out my frustrations, making Brandon more fearful of me at a time when he needed to lean on me. I'll admit, it's highly likely that one of the reasons

Brandon hit other kids at the height of his anxiety was because he picked up that up from me: the habit of dealing with his frustrations through violence. Yet it wasn't exactly possible to reason with a four-year-old, because his ability to think through consequences and understand them was limited.

I understood the importance of discipline falling down like gravity: sudden, clear, and unarguable, with little explanation. But just what form should that take?

Even something as simple as putting him in timeout didn't work, because Brandon refused to sit there. I had watched "Super Nanny" on TV, and tried to follow her advice: she explained that, if a child jumps up from time out, the parent needs to grab him and put him back. But after I grabbed him and put him back, grabbed him and put him back, grabbed him and put him back, over and over and over until I thought I'd lose my mind, I realized that there was no way I could match Brandon's determination to get around this punishment. So, I tried a different tactic: taking away things he loved: mainly computer games. But he was so determined to act out that after a while he seemed to accept this punishment. He would rather lose one of his beloved computer games than give up his coping mechanisms for dealing with anxiety: throwing things, disobeying rules, hitting, screaming, in short, doing anything he could think of to make sure I came back to school to get him.

I hate to admit it but, because we got off on the wrong foot in dealing with the hole that Floyd's absence created in our household, I would just have to keep hammering away at Brandon's behaviors with consistent discipline without hope of results for a *long time*. Because I hadn't understood how to deal with separation anxiety in the beginning, I now had to prove to Brandon that I would not give up on him. In a way, that meant doing just what Super Nanny had suggested, repeating the discipline over and over and over until it stuck. For us, that might not be time outs, but instead promising special outings for good behavior and taking them away for bad behavior. I had to realize that if Brandon acted indifferent to these punishments, that didn't mean it wasn't sinking in. I needed to retrain him, not only to behave or expect consequences, but also to know that, at the end of the day, I would be there for him no matter what.

If I had it to do over again, I would have done more than simply change the way I disciplined Brandon after Floyd left. I would have gone back farther in time, and taken a great role in disciplining Brandon from the beginning. I'd often left that role up to Floyd.

Floyd never hit. In fact, he rarely had to give consequences. The sound of Floyd's voice was enough to stop his son in his tracks and make him behave. "I said do it now!" he would command in a no-nonsense tone. Brandon would turn around and give him an angry scowl, but he would still do whatever Floyd said. That was not the case when I told him what to do.

I tended to simply fuss, not quite as ineffectively as the young baby-talking teachers I mentioned earlier, but not much better either. "Brandon, just do what I tell you… Brandon, stop that now…" I would say in an irritated voice that showed no faith that I could get him to stop. Worse, I might pose a question: "Brandon, what did I tell you?" or "Brandon, why are you doing that?" Questions are not commands, and boy, did Brandon know that!

Part of the problem was that Floyd really was filled with the kind of certainty that I had a hard time duplicating. I simply didn't feel as sure of my ability to maintain control as he did about his. If I had known how important it was, I would have worked harder at it—before Floyd was deployed. The problem was that Brandon knew I could be manipulated, and he played games with me. I wouldn't give in on something, so he'd bargain. Rather than stand there and argue with him, or deal with all his counter-offers, or listen to that whining tone that got under my skin, sometimes I'd meet him halfway—just because I wanted the noise to stop.

"I told you that you couldn't watch TV unless you cleaned your room!"

"I did."

"Your toys are still on the floor."

"I made my bed."

"That's not your whole room. Pick up your toys."

"I'll just watch this show, then pick up my toys."

"No. Pick up your toys now."

"Then can I watch this show?"

"If you pick up your toys."

If you blink, you might miss what went wrong there. The truth was, he'd broken a rule, and should not have been allowed to watch TV at all. Break the law, go to jail. In that moment, he learned that he could get around me.

With Floyd it was "Do what I say and that's that!" There was no discussion. If Brandon tried to argue, Floyd would give more consequences. He didn't dole out the consequences often, but he didn't have to. Brandon learned in two or three tries that they were coming.

If Floyd and I had both been equally firm and no-nonsense in our parenting, then Brandon wouldn't have had the option of manipulating me as part of his way to cope with his father's absence. In some ways I knew that his acting out was his way of telling me that he needed his father and the firmness, reliability, and discipline his father provided. But in another way it was also as if he thought, "Daddy's not here and I wish he were, but at least I can get away with more now."

When Floyd talked to Brandon about leaving, although he gave him the usual instructions that you might expect from a father, "You mind your mother" and all that, it wasn't enough. Given that I was already weaker on discipline, we should have had a family talk in which Floyd passed the disciplinary baton to me. He should have explained that Brandon was to consider my rules Daddy's rules, and to know in no uncertain terms that Daddy would not approve if Brandon disobeyed.

Floyd and I should have had a private discussion, too, to consider the methods of discipline that had worked best up to that point. Since I knew he was more effective at getting results, it would have been to all our benefit for Floyd and I to seriously consider and identify what it was in his approach that worked better than mine, and for us to discuss ways that I could apply it.

Embarrassing as it might have been, it would also have been helpful if I had been willing to ask Floyd to help me identify my weaknesses as a disciplinarian, so that I could make necessary changes. Of course, it wouldn't have been good to have that discussion in front of Brandon, because parents need to keep a united front. If Floyd and I had had such a discussion, I might have gotten a bit defensive, and we might have argued. But it would have been a lot better than dealing with the arguments we had over Brandon later, when Floyd was overseas.

You read that right: Floyd and I often argued about Brandon during our long-distance calls. Don't think separation anxiety is just the child's issue alone. This type of emotional and behavioral problem doesn't exist in a vacuum. Brandon's separation anxiety disorder was partly caused by Floyd's deployment, which affected the whole family. It was also partly caused by all the mistakes we made in trying to deal with Floyd's deployment. And of course, once the separation anxiety settled in for a long stay, it exacerbated all the grief and fear that Floyd and I were already suffering: being separated as a couple and missing each other, both of us fearing that he could die in Afghanistan, him unable to find comfort in his family, me coping with family issues without his support.

When Brandon had intense behavioral issues, Floyd and I talked about it. But, because we were far apart, these conversations offered little relief. I had to deal with Brandon's behavior on my own and I resented Floyd for it—even though the logical part of me knew it wasn't his fault. Floyd was helpless to do anything, which frustrated him, so he became irritable with me for not handling it better—even though the logical part of him knew it wasn't my fault.

Floyd hadn't wanted to leave home in the first place. Not that he wasn't proud of his role in the military; he was. Not that he was facing constant danger; he worked in an office, which was a lot tamer than a field job (although it was still scary because the office was in Kandahar which often took incoming rocket-fire). The bottom line was he didn't want to leave us. This wasn't just my emotional projection. Remember, he was the sensitive one in the relationship. "I don't want to leave you," he'd said on more than one occasion, crying like a baby.

Whether it was healthy or not, he kept repeating that sentiment throughout his deployment, by phone, via emails, on Skype: "I hate being away from you and the boys. I'm just ready to come home. I'm counting down the days." I know he was just expressing himself, but sometimes I wondered if it was good to spend so much time talking about it, because it made it harder to talk to him. Each contact felt like another goodbye, and each new goodbye meant re-experiencing our separation.

When he came home for my surgery, it almost seemed to make the separation harder on him than if he'd just stayed away for the whole year. He cried even harder when he had to leave again. I suppose I could have taken a clue from that, because I think the same was true for Brandon. Each time his father came back, to the car for a few minutes, to the house for a couple of weeks, it only made him freak out even more when Dada had to leave again.

I realize now that the same was probably true, when the daycare providers called me to come talk to Brandon in the middle of the day. Seeing me didn't make it easier, but only harder to watch me leave again. Maybe that's why he often escalated things so far, knowing I would have to take him home.

Floyd tried to help manage our family issues over the phone, he really did. But it wasn't enough. Boy did I let him know it, too. So I guess you could say that in some ways, like Brandon, I was acting out.

"You just left me in the lurch and I have to deal with all this crap by myself," I would whine. "You need to be here. You need to handle this, because I can't do it. I'm tired of this."

"Danielle, you know I don't have any choice. I have to be here. Just hang in there. Everything is going to be all right."

That's when I would lose it—please excuse my language, but I want you to understand how upset I was—shouting things like, "That's easy for you to say! You don't have to spend an extra hour driving back and forth from work to that fucking daycare to deal with these mother-fucking incompetent teachers and find out what the hell our Goddamn boy is doing! Half the time I get there and he's like a crazy person, tearing up the joint. I can't do this shit any more!" I feel guilty just thinking about the way I talked to my husband. What was he supposed to do anyway, all the way in Afghanistan, a place where he could get killed at any moment? Even knowing that, I sometimes dared to think that he had it easier than me. Because no one expected him to control those bombs, but everyone expected me to control our little boy.

Thank God that, although Floyd was the emotional one in the relationship, he was also rock solid—there's probably a lesson in there somewhere. He rarely lost his cool, but just tried to help me see reason. "Stop all that cursing," he'd say. "It's not helping."

Although I'd go on a little longer, after a while I did respond to his calm control, just like Brandon did. "OK, OK. I'm sorry. What do you think I should do?"

Sometimes he had great advice. Other times he had no idea what to do. The best advice he gave me was the simplest: whenever I called him right before dealing with Brandon at the daycare center, he always told me to calm down before I walked inside. "Danielle, don't go in there with an attitude." So I'd sit in the car and take slow, deep breaths for a few minutes before I went into the building. I think it really did make a difference. In a way, it was as if Floyd was in the room with me; he was the one who had helped me calm down, and now I was bringing Floyd's calm certainty to our son, because he could no longer bring it into the space himself.

Sometimes he told me to call him after I picked up Brandon, when I was on my way home. Knowing he would be waiting to talk with me after I dealt with that day's disaster was also a big help. It wasn't the full support I wanted, but it was something, and that was better than nothing.

Sometimes Floyd tried to take pressure off me by suggesting that I call his friend G to watch Brandon. G was pretty available because he didn't have a job, and he seemed glad to help. But it really only solved a small part of the problem. You see, G didn't have a car, so I still had to go to the daycare center to pick Brandon up and drop him off at G's. It wasn't as good a solution as Floyd seemed to think it was. Theoretically, I could go back to work afterward, but sometimes it took so much driving to make this happen that by the time I got back to work there was only an hour left in the workday. What was the point?

Another problem was that Brandon often threw a bigger fit over staying at G's house than he did over staying at the daycare center. "If you would behave at daycare then you wouldn't have to stay at G's house," I said. But he kicked up a fuss until my nerves were frazzled. One day I decided it would be easier to pick up both Brandon and G, and then drive the two of them to our house instead. When I tried that, I picked Brandon up first, and soon I heard him in the backseat crying.

"Why are you crying?" I asked.

"I don't want to go to *G's* house."

"You're not going to *G's* house. I'm going to take you home, and *G's* coming to our house."

"I want to go back to daycare,"

"If you had acted right in the first place, you wouldn't be sitting here," I said.

Looking back, I can see that he was still just trying to figure out how to get unlimited access to his mother at any hour of the day or night. He was still manipulating me. It was hard to reconcile that with the idea that he was also still trying to get me to prove to him that I wasn't going to abandon him. I didn't know how to assure him that I wouldn't abandon him, while still refusing to give in to his manipulations.

Ultimately, *G* was only minimal help. Just because he wasn't working didn't mean he didn't have a life, and some weeks I had to pull Brandon out of daycare early almost every day. I know Floyd was too busy with his own work overseas to have a clear idea of the whole picture. He grew frustrated at what he saw as me making more out of the problem than it was, while I grew frustrated at what I saw as him not recognizing how bad it really was.

Sometimes I tried to bring other male friends of Floyd's into our family circle while Floyd was gone, hoping Brandon would take some comfort in having another man around. I called Floyd's cousin once to see if he'd take Brandon to a ball game, and the cousin was happy to do it. But Brandon wanted nothing to do with it.

"Are you going?" Brandon asked me.

"No, this is just for fellas. I'm just going to hang here."

"I don't want to go," he said.

"Why not?"

"Because you're not going."

You might be tempted to think, "Aw, how sweet." At the beginning I sometimes thought that, too. But it was just too much. Brandon was so dependent on me that he was strangling the emotional life out of me. I desperately needed a break.

It was clear that he wasn't just holding onto me so hard because he missed his daddy, but also because he was afraid I was going to leave, too. Since I had become a single parent of sorts, it wasn't easy for me to calm those fears, because, like many single parents, I often had to leave him in the care of other people.

I remember once I needed to attend a conference, so I asked a girlfriend to take care of him for a couple of days. On the second day she had an emergency, so she had to ask yet another girlfriend to step in and take care of him. I knew that must have been a nerve-wracking situation for a boy with abandonment issues. When I came back on the third day, he looked at me with big, sad, accusing eyes, and asked, "Why you leave me?"

There was really no satisfying way to explain this to a four-year-old, even a four-year-old going on five. The world of adult demands and responsibilities meant nothing to him yet. What's more, I didn't think he should have to understand that world yet. As he asked that question, "Why you leave me?" it was hard not to feel defensive, guilty, defeated, and a little abandoned myself.

If we are honest with ourselves as husbands or wives of military servicemen and women, then I think we can start by admitting this: there is no real way to fill the hole left behind when a loved one disappears from the family for a year at a time. I realized that some aspects of our problem could not be solved, only survived.

A Note to Parents:

Whether a child suffers from typical separation anxiety, severe separation anxiety, or separation anxiety disorder, most professional advice on the subject is aimed at children whose parents haven't actually abandoned them. **Although it's through no real fault of their own, military parents who get deployed do, more or less, abandon their children for weeks, months, and sometimes years at a time.** To a developing child, these time periods don't seem brief in duration or minor in importance. And while some of the advice I've received on the subject has been helpful, I'd like to devote the end of this chapter to well-meaning professional advice that has not worked in our case, and which I've concluded may not apply in the situation of a military child whose father or mother has been deployed.

The following are **a few examples of advice that might be great for most kids suffering separation anxiety, but *not* for children of deployed military parents:**

"Do not show how sad you are whenever you part ways." I disagree. Although it might have been a mistake for Floyd to come back to the car the day he left for Afghanistan, I think that if he had failed to exhibit sadness Brandon might have thought his father didn't care about him, and therefore felt even more abandoned. As for me, I should have shown my emotions more when his father left, so Brandon would have understood that his feelings were natural and that he could feel safe showing them around me. Because I hid my feelings and didn't talk about them, I believe this taught Brandon to use the same strategy. The result was that he acted out his anxiety through violent misbehavior instead of talking through it. On the other hand, I do think it's smart not to become emotional when just dropping a child off for daycare, as that would signal to him or her that there's something to worry about, when there's not.

"Tell your child you're not too far away and that you will see each

other again right after school." This was great advice for me, because it was true and included a promise I could keep. But it offered us no resolution for what Floyd was supposed to say or do—as Brandon was certainly not going to see him right after school, or during any time frame that would be meaningful to a small child.

"Tell your child that while you are away you will keep in touch as often as possible." I don't think this was helpful at all in either my case or Floyd's case. Floyd tried to keep in touch with Brandon, but it only made Brandon more depressed and resentful, because every time he heard his father's voice on the phone or saw his face on the computer screen, it reminded him how far away he was. As for me, whenever I tried to call Brandon or drop by during the day, he only cried harder when I had to leave again. This also reinforced the idea that I was at his beck and call to help him get through the day, instead of teaching him self-reliance. I suppose if I had simply dropped in to see him when he was having a good day, that might have helped wean him from dependence on me. But he had so few good days we had no real chance to test that out.

"Leave a note to your child and put it in your child's lunchbox." That might have been sweet, if only Brandon knew how to read. I suppose I could have left him drawings of hearts or smiley faces, or stickers, or photos. We did try putting a photo of his father up in his cubby so he could see it anytime he wanted, and it had no noticeable effect on his behavior at all.

It seems that a new list of advice for dealing with separation anxiety is in order for military families.

SIX

"I'll Be Home Soon."

In August, as Brandon approached his fifth birthday, the daycare center decided it was time to move him in with the bigger kids, the five-year-olds in room 119. I began to hope that his separation anxiety would fade away along with his toddler-hood. At first it seemed I was right. Almost immediately, the number of panicked calls from teachers started to decrease. I assumed that was because he was growing up, or because of the influence of older kids. But I soon realized that the biggest change was the teacher.

Each day, when I said hello to Miss Ellen (not her real name), I felt a sense of calm settle into my body. That calm seemed to flow directly from her and wrap itself around my son and me. There was something about her voice, which was simultaneously soothing and firm. I felt as if she were in control. I felt as if, so long as both of us did whatever she said, she had the power to make everything OK. Whenever Brandon threatened to lose control, Ellen had this way of using her voice to let him know she would take no nonsense. "No, no, no, Brandon, we're not having that today," she'd say, and he would look right at her and snap out of it, as if he were coming back from the brink of something. "Phew," I thought. "With Ellen on our side, we can finally put the nightmare is behind us."

I envied Ellen's serene, matter-of-fact certainty, and I tried to emulate it. Brandon always had more trouble coping at school than at home, because his separation anxiety was highest when he was separated from both parents. Still, even at home it would be nice to have my son respond to me the way he did to Miss Ellen.

Miss Ellen taught me that firmness and kindness could go hand-in-hand. Not only did Brandon's behavior improve, so did my parenting. Since Brandon spent so much time at daycare, and since my absence from that setting was an issue, teamwork between the teachers and myself was important, and Miss Ellen seemed to understand that best. Together, she and I found ways to keep my son occupied with activities that would stop him from focusing on his anxieties.

Brandon liked to throw things and swing things, both for fun and to alleviate stress. That could be bad if he threw things at other kids. But sometimes Miss Ellen gave him a ball to throw, so long as he threw it away from the other kids. I also signed him up for T-ball, so he could swing a bat and throw a ball. He loved it, and it allowed him to blow off extra steam. When he engaged in those activities, he didn't seem as inclined to tear things up, because he was focusing that same energy on throwing, hitting, and running in a safe way.

Sometimes when I dropped him off, he would start his day with one of the younger, less confident teachers. On those days we often walked into an entire roomful of unruly kids running around in uncontrolled chaos. I felt stressed out just standing there. On those days I thought, "Oh, God. Here we go." Sure enough, those were the days when I'd get called back to the daycare center because Brandon had lost it again.

But when I would come in to talk to him, or to take him home, afterward I usually turned him straight over to Miss Ellen, either when

I left to return to work or when I brought him back in the morning. She took him in-hand instantly: "Brandon, come over here. Let's trace your name," or "Let's do this," or "Let's do that." She always immediately found something to grab his attention and hold it, so that he would have something to focus his energy on besides tearing up the room. One other teacher had a similar effect on him, but Miss Ellen was a sort of miracle worker. She was the one who became my primary role model for how to deal with my son.

I began to study the differences between her methods and the methods of the other teachers—who Brandon often ran right over. One thing I noticed was that the less effective daycare workers talked to my nearly five-year-old son in much the same tone they used with the two- and three-year-olds. If he didn't do as told, or started to yell or throw things, they would say in soft, babyish voices, "Come here, Brandon," or "We don't do that Brandon," or "That's not nice, Brandon." I tried to explain to them, "No, no, I don't want you to baby him anymore. He's a big boy now. You need to insist that he act like one."

Miss Ellen always talked in a way that assumed Brandon knew better and that demanded he live up to that. "Brandon, we're having none of that. Stop it right now." That really helped. She wasn't mean; she was just giving Brandon the structure he needed, which was doubly important to a child who feared the absence of his parents. Brandon needed a feeling of security more than most kids, and part of that security was in knowing that someone was there who would not only protect him from the big bad world, but from himself. He needed boundaries.

I realized that if I set clearer boundaries, that would also help him to feel more secure with me. If I was firm and in control, but also kind and calm in my parenting, then Brandon would begin to learn that he could count on me. His father was gone for a year, but I was still there, and this was my chance to show him that I was sticking like glue—in every way.

So, when he threw fits, I talked to him in the best no-nonsense voice I could muster, "Brandon, you're almost five. You're not a baby anymore. You're a big boy now. It's not acceptable for big boys to scream or hit or throw things."

"I don't want to be a big boy," he said. "I want to be a Transformer. Then I could transform back to a baby."

"No, no, no. That's not possible. You graduated from the baby's class. You're in the big boys' class now. You're not a baby. You're a big boy. You have to act like big boys do. There are lots of good things about being a big boy. You can play more games and do more things."

Sometimes I convinced him. "Yeah. I'm big, strong man," he would say. But other times he continued to insist that he didn't want to grow up.

In many ways, it was the normal struggle of children trying to figure out how to have the best of both worlds: the privileges of growing up, combined with the lack of responsibility of childhood. Yet this normal tug-of-war was more extreme, because of his separation anxieties. When he swung into the phases of hanging onto his babyhood, it wasn't just about irresponsibility, misbehavior, or testing boundaries. Instead, it was a no-holds-barred leap into wanton, destructive, violent defiance.

Although much of his behavior was under control, every now and then he'd remind me that all that anguish was still bubbling under the surface. He continued to find moments to let out his repressed anger over his father's abandonment, his fears over my absence, and his desire to figure out the right crazy-button to push to force us to come back. It often seemed to be working on me. But there was no way for it to work on his father, half a world away in Afghanistan.

Brandon started pre-school in September. At first he seemed excited. But he still had many days when he told me, flat out, "I don't want to go."

My hopes increased when I stopped by his school once in the middle of the day and saw him walking to class. He had a big grin on his face, swung his arms, and looked as relaxed and happy as any other kid. I breathed a small prayer, "Thank You, God."

Things were still precarious, because we were now combining his new environment in preschool with his old environment at the daycare center, where he still spent time before and after school. Now and then he had meltdowns in one location or the other or both. But most days were good.

One thing that seemed to help ease the transition was that I had really learned the value of talking to my son, and had turned it into a ritual. Every day when I picked him up from daycare, I asked, "How was your day, Brandon?" He always looked at me funny, but I ignored this and asked anyway. I knew that it was important to show him that he was important to me, and that he would always be important to me even if he pretended to blow me off. This is how my son tested me, and I was determined to show him that I wasn't so easy to shake off. These were the small steps to turning separation into an ordinary part of a relationship between two people who would always stay connected no matter what.

Sometimes he tried to dodge my questions with, "I'm too tired to talk."

"Well, Momma is just trying to find out how your day went," I said.

"Talk to me later," he said, annoyed.

"OK."

When I tried to talk to him later I might get another, "I'm tired." I wonder if maybe I had unconsciously taught him to dodge sharing his emotional life with me, because I'd become pretty good at doing that myself. But every parent makes mistakes, and that doesn't mean we're forced to live with those mistakes forever. So when he asked, "Why do you keep asking me about my days?" I told him, "I really want to know how you are. I want to know if you had a good day or not." If he still refused, I wasn't above using rewards and punishment to convince him to communicate. "If you want me to buy you things from Game Stop, you're going to need to learn to talk to me about how your days are."

By insisting on communication, what I was really letting him know, over and again, was this: I'm not giving up on you.

Whenever he refused to communicate, I knew those were the times when it was even more important to find out how his days were going. So I was very consistent about talking to his teachers and daycare providers about his behavior, his moods, and his performance.

I remember one pre-school teacher saying, "He's the smartest one in the classroom. He does have a small behavior problem, but I think he's being influenced by some of the other kids in the class." She described some of the unruly behavior of the other children. From her description, I felt certain that those kids also had parents in the military who were deployed overseas. I began to worry about the power of those other kids to affect not only my son's behavior, but also the development of his character. So I had a talk with him about the children he spent time with.

"Brandon, you are not to hang out with those kids who aren't minding the teacher. If other kids want to be bad, you remove yourself. You go to the teacher and you say, "Mr. Harris, they're being bad.""

"Isn't that being a tattle tale?"

"Not when they're trying to get you to act like them. It's OK to tell the teacher."

"OK."

"You don't follow them. You follow you. You follow Brandon."

"OK, I follow Brandon.

Mostly, these kinds of talks seemed to work. He did have lingering problems that might be associated with separation anxiety: always wanting to be the center of attention in the classroom, having a "me, me, me" and "gimme, gimme" attitude, always wanting to have what the other kids had and wanting to do what the other kids did.

One time the kids were playing a letter game, and when one little girl took her turn she used the letters he wanted to use. He got so angry he started crying. I'd like to point out here, that he's the baby of our family. In fact, since Floyd's son Damien isn't around all the time, Brandon often enjoys the role of an only child. So, although I can't say I've spoiled him, it wouldn't be a stretch to say that he's used to the lion's share of attention at home. As a kid with separation anxiety disorder, that need for attention might simply have been heightened. When Mommy and Daddy weren't around, it may have become his way of proving that he was still important.

Brandon and I talked about that, too. It remained an issue, but at least he was listening. There seemed to be hope that he could learn to overcome his behavioral problems.

As time went on, when Brandon felt a tantrum coming on, he learned, perhaps subconsciously, to give me a verbal warning. He was learning to verbalize his feelings, though it was slow going.

One day when we arrived at daycare, he stated quite simply, "I want to go home."

"No, Brandon, you have to stay here because Momma has to work. I have to work so I can make money to go to Game Stop and buy you all these little games that you want."

Even though he loved Game Stop, this tactic wasn't working anymore. "I want to go to work with you."

"No Brandon. Little boys aren't allowed at my job."

I saw his face scrunch up in that way that set off an alarm in me. So I stayed for a few minutes and followed him around the room as he walked from place to place. Once again, I suggested we go into the motor skills room, where he grabbed these twirly toys and started twirling them. He grabbed a few other things, and aggressively played with one after another. When I figured he'd blown off enough steam, I said, "Are you OK now?"

"Yes," he said, in a tense voice that made it obvious he was lying.

But this time, I called him on it. There was not going to be any more hiding our feelings in this family. "Brandon, you are not OK. You are not. You seem angry to me. Do you want to talk about it?" He wasn't ready to say anything. But I think it was important that he knew I was willing to listen, and that he knew that I saw emotions in him that maybe he didn't. I waited with him a little longer and then said, "Well, Mommy has to go to work. I'll be back for you later."

When I walked out, I turned back to watch him through the window. He started kicking tables and chairs, charged around knocking things off the shelves, and hit another kid. But here was the biggest problem: Miss Ellen wasn't there, and the other teachers weren't even trying to stop him. I sighed and went back into the room.

I walked straight up to Brandon, and in what I thought was a calm, firm voice said, "No, Brandon, you can't be kicking the chairs. There are other kids in here—you can't hit these kids. You're a big boy now, and this is not acceptable behavior."

Sometime in the midst of that, Miss Ellen came through the door. I heard her say to another teacher, "You had to call the mom?"

"No. She was dropping him off, but she never left because Brandon is in one of his moods," the other teacher said.

This ticked me off a little, as I thought, *if only you would have taken charge, I could have left.*

Then Miss Ellen walked up to Brandon and solved everything instantly. "Brandon, are you OK today?"

He shook his head.

At first that hurt my feelings, because he was willing to tell the truth to her, but not to me. Then I realized this was a breakthrough: Brandon was willing to tell the truth to *someone*, he was willing to admit that he wasn't OK. Maybe not to me, but then I was the one he was afraid would abandon him. I would have to give him more time to learn that I wasn't going to do that.

"So, you're having a bad morning, Brandon," Miss Ellen acknowledged. Then she quickly moved on. "You want some breakfast?"

"Yeah," he said. And that was the end of it.

When I came back that afternoon, I asked, "Miss Ellen, what did he do when I left?"

"Brandon was fine."

"I don't understand. This morning he didn't want me to leave. I was sure he'd throw a fit. What is it you're doing right that I'm doing wrong?"

She smiled. "Don't worry. You're doing the right thing. You're his mother, and I'm his teacher. We have a different understanding. But if you weren't doing the right thing, he wouldn't be doing better." She confirmed that my talking to him *was* helping.

I knew it would be easier to solve the whole thing if only he could talk to his father, too. It was certainly an option. We had a Skype connection online and I talked to Floyd by computer several times a week, face-to-face and everything. We also talked by phone now and then. But, even though Floyd was the very person Brandon wanted most, he refused to speak to him. Sometimes, if I bribed Brandon with promises of toys or treats, he would talk to his father for a couple of minutes, but he rarely said more than a few words.

One time I asked him why he didn't want to talk to his Dada, and he said, "I'm going to beat Dada up."

"Why are you going to beat him up?

"Because he's not here."

"OK. So you're angry. Let's talk about that."

"No!"

"It's OK to be angry."

"Leave me alone!"

Though it was important to talk to him about his feelings, I still had to learn not to push him farther than he was prepared to go. A few times when I insisted on talking to him about his father, he tried to hit me. I wondered if he was just as mad at me as he was at his father. Maybe he thought I'd done something to run his father off. I didn't know. This was another situation in which spending more time with a therapist might have been good for me.

Then came the moment when the father-son bond seemed to get both better and worse at the same time. Floyd had an idea that was either the most inspired or the most ignorant thing either of us had attempted yet: he started sending home DVD's of himself, in which he talked directly to his son and read him a story. I remember staring at Brandon as he watched his father reading *Curious George*, and it struck me that I'd never seen him so mesmerized. It was as if nothing else existed except his father's face and voice. It was so odd, after all those times he refused to talk to his daddy. I didn't get it.

Then, on Brandon's birthday, a third video arrived. In that one Floyd said something he hadn't said in the other videos: "Dada will be home soon." I froze. We had told Brandon the same thing before, but he had no concept of the word "soon." I thought we'd been telling Brandon the truth, but I wondered if, from Brandon's point of view, it had become our greatest lie to him. I hoped that maybe he wouldn't focus on that part of the video.

No such luck. It became all Brandon could talk about: "Dada said he'll be home soon!" He was floating on a cloud all day. That night when

Floyd called, I said, "You told him you'd be home soon. Do you think you should have said that? Because now that's all he talks about. I'm worried about what's going to happen when week after week goes by and you're still not here."

Floyd admitted that he hadn't considered that, and he apologized, but he also said, "I'm sure it'll be fine. I don't think that one sentence is going to ruin our son. And I *will* be home soon. When I do come back he'll realize I was telling the truth."

But the sickening feeling wouldn't leave the pit of my stomach. All that day, Brandon kept repeating to his older brother, Damien, "Brother, Dada said he'll be home soon!"

"Good, good," Damien said. "We'll be here waiting on him."

Brandon was so cheerful that I began to believe maybe his father hadn't made a mistake. If only I could keep putting a positive spin on it, "Yes, Daddy will be home soon. Soon."

But deep down, I knew that "soon" was going to drag on and on. Maybe Brandon would be able to keep his behavior together, maybe he wouldn't. But I knew that his emotional health was in danger. I was almost more afraid that he would stop showing his feelings altogether, that they would dive down so deep that my lively, spirited son would be lost forever.

Brandon wasn't the only one emotionally affected by the word "soon." Both of us began to turn giddy with hope at the sound of that word. I began to see Floyd everywhere, and so did Brandon.

Both of us associated uniforms with Floyd. Whenever Brandon saw a man in uniform, he would point and say, "Dada." Not wanting to give him false hope, I frequently pretended not to notice these walking reminders of the missing man of our house. But one day, shortly after Floyd said he'd be home soon, I was sitting in the car with Brandon going through our now daily before-school talk, and I saw a boy that looked like one of Brandon's friends walking with his father, a soldier.

I said, "Hey, there's Neil (not his real name) and his Dad."

Within seconds, I heard sniffling from the back seat.

I turned around. "What's wrong, Brandon?"

"I want Dada."

I turned away from him. Thinking I'd made a mistake by pointing out a man in uniform, I compounded it by making another mistake: *I changed the subject.*

If I could have that moment back, I probably wouldn't point out the man in uniform in the first place. But if I couldn't resist mentioning it, I wouldn't turn my back on Brandon's tears. I would turn to Brandon and say, "It's OK to want your dad. It's OK to cry. Sometimes I see a dad walking with his son and I miss Dada, too."

Sometimes I was so busy wallowing in guilt over the damage I might be doing to my son, that I continued to lose sight of my son. If I was going to help get both of us through this, I needed to learn to accept that this whole situation was a mess, and there was no tidy way out of it.

A Note to Parents:

Psychologists who are experts on separation anxiety point out the importance of being honest with your children about separation. They say that before any separation it's important not to hide from children what's going to happen, that during a separation it's important not to hide your feelings, and that throughout all of it you must encourage children to be honest about their feelings. If this were easy to do, we would never have had a problem. I think all of us, Floyd, Brandon, and I, were willing to be honest about our feelings. We just didn't understand how to do that, or to what extent.

Here's the dilemma with being honest about separation with a four- to five-year-old child: he's unable to imagine exceptionally long times and distances, he's unable to imagine the complex problems that require adults to leave from time to time, and he's unable to fully understand his own emotional life or the emotional life of those around him.

Brandon was barely starting to grasp the days of the week, much less the length of a year. **To him, the word "soon" referred to anything from minutes, to hours, to days. So when Floyd said, "I'll be home soon," though it was true from his perspective, it would soon be revealed as a lie from Brandon's perspective.** Floyd wasn't coming home in a few minutes, hours, or days. His return was still months away. It might as well have been another year, as far as Brandon could tell. We were stretching our son's trust beyond normal limits. When I agreed with Floyd, "Yes, Dada will be home soon," I too became a big fat liar. No wonder Brandon wanted to hit me.

I think that's where learning to live with the messiness of separation can come in handy. If I had been more honest about my feelings, it would have mattered less whether my explanations made sense. It might be hard to explain the adult complications of war, or time, or distance to a child. But kids can sense when you're being straight with them. If I had just made it clear over and again, in so many words, "This sucks, and you deserve to feel sad and angry, and Mommy feels sad and angry too," Brandon would have gotten the idea.

Though I'd begun talking to Brandon about his feelings, I still feared the most emotional moments. And I had yet to talk about my own feelings. Though I had stopped yelling and hitting, I was still in the "do as I say, not as I do" mode of parenting.

I kept forgetting that it wasn't just Floyd's absence that scared Brandon. It was the possibility that I was next. If I was hiding my feelings, you can bet he sensed it. So how could he trust me not to be hiding something else—maybe some secret plan to leave the country, too?

On the other hand, families get separated from each other many times in life. That's reality. It isn't enough just to be there for a child. **We need to model for them that they can survive separation and scary feelings, and show them how to do that, by doing it ourselves—with calm, strength, honesty, and the willingness to reach out to others for support.**

SEVEN
Change Has Its Own Clock

While a brief time in the life of an adult can seem longer to a child, sometimes the reverse is also true: what is a brief stage in the life of a child, can seem like forever to an adult. Although I hoped Brandon would stop acting out as soon as his father's year in Afghanistan was up, to me this one year in our lives seemed to be stretching into an eternity. Sometimes I wondered if maybe the counselors, teachers, and I had all been fooled—if maybe my clever son was just using his father's absence as an excuse to run amok. He never did seem to go through the terrible twos I'd always heard about. Maybe this was one of those developmental milestones he'd missed and now he was making up for it.

After all, I had tried all the methods of dealing with separation anxiety that I had learned from my brief stint with Brandon's therapist, my own therapist, a revolving door of school counselors, and the occasionally well-trained teacher. Not to mention informational brochures and online guidelines put together by experts, and even common sense advice from my mother, sisters, and husband. Yet my son was still suffering from bouts of violent tantrums, drawn-out crying fits, and wild defiance.

I was smart enough not to take any chances. He was having more good days than he had early on, but I didn't take that for granted. I feared that if I let up on any of our new routines, we might lose all the progress we'd made. So, I kept following the most sensible of the advice I'd picked up in recent months. The two primary things I worked hardest at to help us get through this tough time were: 1) our daily talks, and 2) trying to stick to a dependable routine.

To me our talks were a way of taking the temperature of what I called the ticking bomb. That is, the thing eating away inside Brandon that threatened to explode at unpredictable moments and throw our lives off-kilter. We talked both in the morning and after school, but mornings seemed the most critical. That was the toughest time for Brandon. I didn't know why. Probably because morning was when he had to deal with separating from me each day. Simple enough. Yet why his fear of that moment never went away was beyond me. I always showed up again at the end of the day. But then, his father had always been there every day for the previous year, until one day, for no reason Brandon could understand, he wasn't. How could I prove to him that I would never do the same thing? Only time would tell.

Our morning talk and his daily routine were tied tightly together. My counselor had told me not only to maintain the routine, but also to daily remind him what that routine was, so that he would learn to trust me. "Tell him every day what the steps in his day are going to be." It was important to name not just the highlights, but every single predictable step. So each morning, although it felt silly at first, I'd start the day with the same litany:

"It's time to wake up now Brandon. Then we're going to get you dressed, we're going to have breakfast, we're going to get in the car, and I'm going to take you to daycare." It didn't end there. "When you walk through the doors at daycare, this is what you're going to do: you're going to sit down and you're going to draw your name, then you're going to play with toys, then you're going to take a nap, then you'll have an afternoon snack, and then you'll play outside until I come back.

But it didn't work. Or at least, it didn't seem to work. Brandon would nod at the list as if he understood. Yet, he often replaced the routine I described with his own routine: as we drove to school his anxiety would build, when we arrived he would either beg me to stay or ask to come with me, he would pretend to accept my reassurances that I'd be back later, and then, not long after I left, he'd throw a fit, knowing I'd be forced to come back.

I tried to use our talking time on the way to school to get him to let it out. When I saw his face get that tense look on the way to school, I asked him, "What's wrong, Brandon?"

"I don't know."

When we got to school, I'd go with him to the motor growth room and watch him play for a few minutes, suggesting to him, "Get it out, Brandon! I can tell you're upset, so let's shake it out, get moving. Run around. Holler if you need to."

But he would still wait until after I left to blow up.

I kept thinking, "These talks aren't getting us anywhere. Explaining his routine isn't helping. Showing him that I'm there for him at the beginning and end of the day is pointless. Nothing is happening." But I realize now that *it probably* was *working, and I just was too impatient for results.*

I thought Brandon was the one who didn't believe that his father was ever coming back, and who didn't trust that I would come back either. Yet I was the one who didn't believe, who didn't trust, who felt afraid. I feared that Brandon was the one who had gone away and might never come back. My trust in him was down, too.

In my worry, it didn't occur to me that, even though he repeated the behavior over and again, the repetition did begin to decline. The changes were so small that it was hard to have hope. And his progress was inconsistent. Uphill progress usually is. It might be weeks before he'd take a step forward, and then another, and then he might slide back. But, by his fifth birthday, he was having fewer tantrums. So I suppose it was working, at Brandon's pace, not mine.

I began to notice that naptime was often the hardest time of all. Maybe that was because falling asleep meant giving up the possibility of control, giving up the possibility of doing something to force my return. Or maybe falling asleep meant the fear of waking up to find I wasn't there. Whatever it was, that was often the time when I'd have to return and explain his routine again:

"Brandon, you know these are your steps. You're going to take a nap. Then you're going to get up and you're going to have snack and you're going to go outside. Then mommy's going to come get you."

"No. Want to go with you now."

One of the teachers suggested that I point at the clock and say, "When the little hand points at the four, that's when I'm coming."

But when I told him that, he looked at the clock, then looked back at me, and said, "But you're here now. Let's go now"

"Yes, but I'm leaving to go back to work. When the hand hits four o'clock, when it hits that four, that's when I'll be back to pick you up."

Other parents reading this may recognize the frustration, and the apparent pointlessness, of explaining our actions to a child. Of course, there are schools of thought that suggest we shouldn't explain ourselves too much, but just lay down the rules and let the child know that he must comply. But my son was in such extreme distress that none of the usual rules were helping. He couldn't cope with the lack of control. He couldn't cope with seeing me leave again. So if I didn't give him some tools to understand what was happening, he was just going to pitch a fit until the teachers couldn't take it anymore.

Again, this was simply a phase in Brandon's young life, a phase brought on by his father's unexpected departure, but a phase nonetheless. It just seemed like forever, because, just as my son had no way of knowing if his father would ever return, I had no guarantees my son was ever going to stop acting out. Brandon was not going to process this problem on my clock, but on his. The things I was saying to him *were* sinking in, but he just needed to hear it *a lot* of times for it to stick. He was getting better, but very, very slowly.

If Brandon's father had died, would I have expected him to completely move on in less than a year as if nothing had happened? Brandon had no way to be sure that wasn't the case. Even the DVDs that Floyd sent didn't prove anything. They weren't flesh and blood, but merely recordings. The thing was, as hard as it was to deal with my son's meltdowns, if I had stopped our routine, or stopped our daily talks, or stopped laying out the expectations for each day, it probably would have been worse. If I had left Brandon hanging, with no explanation, no communication, nothing to depend on—I risked him spending more than just a year in this state of fear. He might have spent the rest of his life unable to cope with separation.

The unfortunate thing was that, as a military family, sometimes the very tools we used to help us get through Floyd's deployment actually worked against us. Brandon had seemed to be getting better, until he received those three DVD's of his father reading and talking to him.

It's difficult to measure the importance to a child of seemingly insignificant moments in their daily routines at home. Floyd and I had always been affectionate with Brandon, giving him plenty of hugs and kisses and regularly saying, "I love you." But Floyd is a bigger hugger than I am; when my husband hugs me, I get a little squirmy after a bit. I suppose Brandon paid close attention to all that.

Even during Floyd's first deployment, when Brandon was two,

Brandon used to get a little clingy with me, following me around and holding my legs. But it wasn't all that noticeable at the time because it can be normal for a two-year-old to be attached to his mommy. I had failed to notice that after Floyd came home that first time, Brandon always seemed relaxed, all three of us did. He didn't cling to either of us, just wandered from room to room: let's see what Dada's up to, OK now let's see what Mommy's up to. They did things together, but not everything. How could I have predicted how important that apparently casual connection really was?

I can see now that the simple reassurance of knowing that his dad was downstairs, and that he could pop in on him anytime he wanted, was important. Just knowing that this man and this woman were living, breathing, and moving around him, in the same house, day-after-day, played a significant role in his childhood development. The significance of all that ordinary daily contact wasn't clear until it was disrupted.

Getting left at home with the slightly less demonstrative parent, and the slightly less patient parent—that was just Brandon's bad luck. I remember when Floyd would say, "Come here, son," and give Brandon a hug, and Brandon would jump in and give the hug but then quickly back off. I guess he was mimicking me, but that doesn't mean he didn't want or need those hugs. I can see now that was just the way a developing child gravitates between attachment and independence, testing the waters of both.

Whenever Floyd wrote or called, that deep affection was still there in his voice and in his words, both to me and to Brandon: "How's my son? … I miss my little buddy… What's my little buddy doing?" But of course Brandon could feel the difference. Heck, I could feel the difference. This had become a long-distance relationship, and everyone knows that's not as good as being up close and in person—period.

Brandon not only took after me in his slightly less demonstrative nature, but also in being an introvert. Not that I'm unfriendly, or even shy, but I'm just not as gregarious as Floyd. I don't feel as much of a need or desire to have a lot of friends, to go out and socialize, or to be around a lot of people. In the same way, I noticed that, while some kids at school seemed to always be surrounded by friends, Brandon was one of those who were content to spend a lot of one-on-one time with just one or two friends. Maybe it should have occurred to me that a child who depends so heavily on a small group of people would suffer more when one member of his sphere is missing.

Not only did that probably make it even harder on him when Floyd left, it also made it harder for him to recover—because he had a smaller circle of people he was willing to turn to for comfort. My son was close friends with two boys in daycare. But he was closest to the boy I mentioned earlier, the one I called Neil. Brandon and Neil did everything together. It was sweet, but it was also problematic, because Neil became one of the people who helped keep Brandon calm at school. So long as Neil was at daycare when I dropped Brandon off, he seemed to have an easier time coping when I left. But Neil wasn't always there first thing in the morning.

"Where's Neil?" Brandon would ask in a worried voice.

"Neil's coming. He'll be here soon."

I suppose that comment was too strong an echo of what we'd said about Floyd, who had yet to return. So Brandon's face would twist into a mask of anger.

I tried to ease his fears. "Neil will be here. About ten minutes after I leave, Neil will be here."

But even though Neil did appear a short time later, Brandon's anxiety was already heightened. That was a day when he'd be more likely to have a meltdown. Looking back, I suppose it would have been helpful if, long before Floyd was deployed, I had worked harder to surround Brandon with more people—both more extended family and more friends. That way losing one person from his routine might have been less devastating, and he would have had a larger support system to deal with it. But I'm not sure how I would have managed it, because my family and Floyd's family lived far away, and because I wouldn't want to force my son to make more friends than it was in his nature to make.

It also might have helped if Floyd and I had made more friends with other military families. Although Floyd had plenty of friends in his unit, the army teamwork touted in military brochures and ads applies more to work out in the field. It didn't apply as much to the social life of military families—at least it didn't at Floyd's post. There were few opportunities to get together with other military families, and most of those gatherings were about planning "welcome home" parties or things like that.

I could have used some sort of parent support group, where I might have met mothers going through similar experiences and gotten advice. Maybe I could have set up play dates with them and their children, to expand my son's list of playmates, as well as my own circle of friends. Looking back, I suppose that maybe I could have tried to create a group on my own. But I was so busy just surviving that it wasn't something I thought about.

There were probably limits on how much it might have helped to do things differently. Some of Brandon's suffering was inevitable under the circumstances. If our son's development was dealt a blow, that only made sense, because an important component of his development had been taken away: the consistency of his family and home life. I could talk to him about it all day, but no amount of talking was going to get Brandon to smack his hand to his head and say, "Oh, right, I get it now: it's a great thing to have my father vanish for a year!"

As it was, just about the time I thought we were moving from survival mode to improvement mode, that was when we received that DVD in which Floyd said, "Dada will be home soon!" With that, we were back in survival mode. When Dada didn't come home that day, or the next, Brandon did finally lose it. This time he didn't break down at the daycare center, but instead at the school where he attended pre-kindergarten.

He'd been showing a lot of improvement since starting school. In fact, for the first month, although Brandon had some typical adjustment issues, his teacher told me he was doing great—until after he saw that birthday video. Then one day Brandon threw a tantrum in class, his first one outside the daycare environment. So I could no longer just blame the lack of expertise of the daycare workers—though now I was tempted to blame the lack of training that both teachers and childcare professionals seemed to have in this subject.

Then again, maybe they were relying on the only information available to them on the problem, which was very little. The connection between military deployment and separation anxiety disorder in children is only now making it onto the radar of educators. Who knew our country would be involved in so many extended conflicts that teachers might need to train for this kind of problem in a classroom? In fact, it's possible that some kids with this problem might need to be in a special classroom setting. For now, there is no such setting.

Several weeks after the arrival of the "Dadda will be home soon" DVD, Brandon continued to cave in, switching from enraged tantrums to tearful emotional breakdowns. One day, when the bus driver dropped the kids off at our stop, the man paused to talk to me. He told me Brandon had a meltdown at school. In fact, my son was still crying when he got off the bus.

We asked him, "What's making you so upset, Brandon? Why are you crying?"

I was shocked at his response. He lifted his head and hollered at the top of his lungs, "I want my daddy! I want my daddy!" Then his shoulders slumped down, and his head dropped, like a man defeated in a prizefight.

He broke down in tears many times after that video came. When I saw how it affected him, I cried, too.

* * *

In between meltdowns, Brandon was still learning. One thing he was learning at pre-school was how to tell time on a clock, and the days of the week, and the months of the year. So, I began trying to explain to him how much time would pass until his father was coming home. One day he asked me to show him on the calendar what day his dad was coming home, and when I showed that to him and counted the days in between, that seemed to comfort him. It didn't last. He soon grew depressed again. When he continued to come home depressed, we started to mark the passing of the days on the calendar.

Floyd's older son, Damien, had his own issues dealing with his father's absence. At 13, he acted out sometimes, too. But it was easy to say to Damien, "Your daddy's got 53 more days and he'll be home." Brandon couldn't count that high yet. Still, he could count to thirty, so when Floyd had a month left in his tour, I told Brandon, "Today your father has just thirty days left, so we're going to count backwards every day, OK? And when we get to zero, that's when we're going to go get Dada." The next day, I'd say, "So, now your father has 29 days left." He picked up on it after a few days, "Now Daddy has 25 days, right?"

If Brandon was new to counting, he was an old hand at identifying familiar places. And whenever we passed an airport, he would start talking about going to get Daddy. One day, we dropped Floyd's cousin off at the airport, and when we started to drive away Brandon said, "Why are we leaving? We have to wait for Dada."

"Dada's not coming today, Brandon. Remember? We're not at zero yet. And when we pick up Dada we won't come to the airport, we'll go back to the gym, the same place where we dropped him off before he left."

Although it hurt my heart to have to go through this over and over, I could see that we'd made progress, because Brandon simply said, "OK," and went back to playing his game.

As the thirty-day countdown to zero was upon us, I began to look back over the painful year Brandon and I had survived. I had to admit that, in spite of the wringer Brandon's separation anxiety had put us through, we'd both managed to grow. Brandon was having a lot fewer tantrums, and when he did they were less about violent acting out and more about tears and asking for what he wanted. As heartbreaking as it was, Brandon screaming, "I want Daddy!" at the top of his lungs was a breakthrough. After so many months of saying "I don't know" every time I asked him what was wrong, now he knew what he wanted and how to say it. That was real progress. Brandon was learning to express his feelings without tearing up a room. And he wasn't going to the other extreme either, pretending everything was OK when it wasn't.

Brandon was learning to count, and he was learning to ask questions. He was learning not to mimic the bad behavior of other kids, but to follow the behavior I'd laid out for him. The teachers used to tell me that my little introvert was a follower. But I continued to repeat the same advice to him: "You've got to be a leader Brandon! You don't follow what other kids do. You follow Brandon!" And he kept repeating it back: "I follow Brandon!" As time passed, he didn't just say it, he started to do it—avoiding other kids who misbehaved and choosing his own way.

He was learning the idea that actions have consequences. I would say, "When you have good behavior, Brandon, what happens?"

"I can get things. I can do things."

"And when you're behavior is not good, what happens then?"

"I get things taken away. I can't go to Game Stop."

I'm only sorry that the counselors had to explain to me not to call him a bad boy, but just to talk about bad behavior. I had heard this before, but "bad girl/good girl" and "bad boy/good boy" was just the kind of language I'd heard growing up and it was a hard habit to break. I felt embarrassed about this early rookie mistake, but I tried to be grateful that least I was able to learn something new. At least I made the change.

A lot of the problem has been that, at the same time I was learning about separation anxiety I was also learning some ordinary lessons about being a parent. Remember, Brandon is my only child. I love my stepson Damien, but I didn't have to raise him from the time he was a baby. So, this was new territory, and being able to tell the difference between what was normal four-year-old behavior and what was separation anxiety wasn't always easy. It also wasn't easy to tell the difference between the kind of responses I needed to give him because he was a *kid*, and the kind of responses I needed to give him because he was a *kid in crisis*.

And let's not forget: I had to deal with all this while suffering my own crisis. Remember, I was desperately missing Floyd, too.

As I said, Brandon wasn't the only one who grew. I did, too. Not only as a parent, but also as a woman. Like Brandon, before Floyd left that second time, I used to be more of a follower. But having to face this crisis with Brandon, I discovered leadership qualities in myself that I didn't know I possessed. Because so many teachers, counselors, and experts couldn't solve Brandon's problem, I often had to take the lead in coming up with strategies and asking for assistance. If we were going to affect Brandon's behavior, we all had to be on the same page, and my maternal instincts took the lead: I was the one who was going to write that page. He was my son. Who else was going to take the lead in helping him if I didn't?

In many ways we were in new territory. Therapy has a lot to say about separation anxiety in children from normal households, or even households where death or divorce is part of the picture. But I found very little information that addressed separation anxiety in terms of military households. So, for example, a DVD from Daddy saying, "I'll be home soon," might have worked well in a regular household, but in a military household the language was problematic. Even for an adult, there's nothing "soon" about a yearlong deployment. When a soldier goes to active duty in a war zone, there's nothing certain about that either. So, I had to lead my family through new territory, where expert advice was only partly helpful. In some ways, I had to become my own expert.

The most important, and most unexpected, lesson I learned about leadership was that *asking for help is not a weakness, but a strength.* As much as I had to lead, I also had to lean on others: the very teachers, counselors, boss, family, and husband who I thought didn't get it. But they each had their own gifts, advice, and assistance to bring to the table, and a lot of it helped. The main thing they offered was the reminder that doing this by myself was impossible.

By watching my son suffer as a consequence of not expressing his feelings, I also learned that a leader doesn't have to pretend everything's OK when it's not. I've learned that it's important to talk about my feelings, rather than hold everything in. I've also learned to let my husband in more, to show him that I wasn't able to do everything without him. I used to think he would criticize me if I didn't stand as strong as a rock while he was gone. I discovered the opposite: that admitting the important role he played in our lives and turning to him for advice made our relationship stronger.

I used to think that what Floyd liked about me was that I was a strong, take-charge kind of woman, and I was afraid to be anything less for fear he might not look at me the same way. I realize now that a truly strong person turns to others for input, help, and support. Leaders don't do it all themselves, sometimes they rely on teamwork, or they delegate. The more I've learned to do that, the stronger I've become. So, instead of respecting me less, Floyd respects me more. He respects me for advocating for our son and for figuring out when I need to stand up to others. But he also respects me for recognizing when I need to turn to others for help.

The ability to lead the way through my son's crisis has given me new confidence to lead in other areas of my life: I've renewed my commitment to getting my degree in business administration, I've taken on more leadership roles at work, and I've had the courage to take on new professional projects—such as writing this book.

My son has grown along with me. I've learned the hard way that he watches all I do. After all we've been through, I now see that I'm finally teaching him to be a leader.

A Note to Parents:

If you're doing everything you can to help your child and the behaviors aren't changing, don't give up hope. While the ongoing behavior might drive you up the wall, the truth is that your messages probably are sinking in. **When a child has been traumatized, it can just take a bit longer for them to respond to corrections.** It's about rebuilding trust, and that takes time.

When I was talking with Brandon about his feelings and his behavior, sometimes it felt as if I was talking to a brick wall. But something was seeping in. The changes were just happening so slowly that I didn't notice them until I had some distance and could look back at them over time. I wanted to see progress on day one, or at least in week one. But it took me six months.

So keep the faith—not just faith in God, though that can help—but faith in yourself and your child and the process. Keep applying the principles that promote consistency and trust in your routine and in your relationship, and have patience. The results will come.

But, because this is a long, tough row to hoe, don't suffer through it alone. Don't think you have to be Wonder Woman, or Superman. You're a human, and the strongest of humans get that way by seeking support. **Create a network of support among family, friends, teachers and coworkers**. Let your boss know what's going on, and be ready to offer valuable work in return for their understanding. A smart boss will know that supporting you through this time will earn back your loyalty, teamwork, and dedication.

Unfortunately, although Floyd's dad and my mom were happy to help when they could, his dad lives in Tennessee and my mom lives in Louisiana. They were just too far away for me to turn to them on a regular basis. I did turn to Floyd's friends, but I had neglected to cultivate enough of my own friends. Part of the problem was that, when I moved home from overseas I slid into the role of wife, mother, and employee, and didn't work at creating social connections.

If I had it to do again, I would have asked for even more help: making more local friends, approaching other military spouses to create a support group, maybe asking my family to visit more often, seeking babysitters to give me a needed break, and more.

Because Brandon had so many issues, I was afraid to leave him with babysitters or neighbors, because I didn't know anyone well enough to trust them with my son. If I left him at home with a babysitter, so that I could catch a movie with a girlfriend, I would spend the whole time worrying about what was happening to Brandon at home. It would have been smart to establish a routine of leaving Brandon with a babysitter now and then before Floyd ever even left, so they would have become familiar to my son. Of course, I couldn't predict that I needed to work at separation anxiety prevention. But I now think that every military family should work at these preventative measures. The risk is so high.

EIGHT

Will Floyd Come Marching Home?

When Brandon acted bored and disinterested during his father's phone calls home, sometimes I wondered if Brandon was punishing him for his absence, or if he was just trying to protect himself emotionally by pretending he didn't care. I suspect both of those things were true to some extent. On the other hand, maybe he was just reacting to the obvious: a cold plastic phone receiver emitting a tiny reproduction of a man's voice was a poor substitute for a daddy in the flesh.

Maybe only adults have the conversational skills required to connect with another human by phone. Small children don't seem to want or need to engage in the kind of back-and-forth communication that requires long strings of questions and replies to keep it going. What kids want are smiles, laughter, a lap to sit on, arms to hold them, hands to swing them around. None of that is available on a phone.

When they did talk, Floyd asked Brandon a lot of questions about what he did all day, but Brandon showed little curiosity about what his father did all day. Looking back, that seems pretty normal. He was still at an age when the idea of what Dada and Mama did when they weren't with him was a mystery he rarely thought about. In our case, that was probably a blessing. If Brandon had a better understanding of words like army, soldier, war, and deployment, he might have suffered more anxiety over his father's absence, and less trust in my promises that Dada would return soon. Not that Floyd was in exceptional danger, but if we'd had to explain that to Brandon it would have been difficult. Floyd did sometimes tell his son that he worked in an office and that he often drove a supply truck.

A few times during their conversations, sirens went off in the background. Brandon would ask, "What's that?"

"The sirens went off."

"Why did sirens go off?"

"People were in town shooting."

"Shooting guns?" Brandon asked, sounding more curious than frightened.

"Yes," Dada said.

That seemed to satisfy Brandon, perhaps because the idea of guns was vague, and Dada didn't ever sound worried. I don't think Brandon ever put together the ideas of guns or Dada with the ideas of danger or death. As a four- to five-year-old child who had never experienced a death, I doubt he thought about death much or had a full grasp of its meaning.

My past experience working with the military in war zones made it a little easier for me to deal with Floyd's deployment without fearing constantly for his life. I'd seen first-hand how well everything in a military compound is fortified. I'd seen and sometimes worn the protective gear soldiers have to don during an emergency. I knew that even when my husband was driving a truck he only drove it inside the compound, which was the size of a small city. Since Floyd primarily had an office job, did not drive a truck outside the perimeter, and did not participate in patrols or other missions in the field, he really was reasonably safe.

It's probably lucky for Brandon that I was a former soldier, and was therefore calmer about Floyd's deployment to a war zone than many spouses are. As freaked out as Brandon was by his father's absence, it might have been worse if I had been constantly worried that Floyd might never return. Seeing that anxiety in me might have driven my sensitive son over the edge.

On the other hand, in a war zone, danger and death are never far away. So that stress probably added to all the others nagging at Floyd's mind, and mine, which Brandon was bound to pick up on. Active duty soldiers do die, even when they're not on patrol, even when they're inside a safe perimeter, even when they're tucked away in an office shuffling papers.

I often think about other families whose parents work outside the perimeter, running patrols and missions, engaging in battle and gunfire, dealing with the constant threat of roadside bombs and insurgent attacks. Imagine a child who suffers separation anxiety because he fears that his father or mother might never come home—only to be told that, yes, after all the promises that Dada or Mommy would return, in fact they really are never coming home. Imagine a child like Brandon spending the rest of his life coming to terms with the fact that his worst fears were true. Imagine a child who is already suffering extreme separation anxiety suddenly being forced to cope with the death of a parent.

I don't think Brandon associated his father going to Afghanistan with the idea of the battles he sometimes saw in video games or on TV. I think that Brandon considered Floyd's job with the military an ordinary job. As far as he knew, all daddies and mommies did work of some sort, some of them wore uniforms to work, and only they knew what they did when they were there. It was part of the adult world about which he knew little and cared less.

Brandon had a vague idea that Dada had gone far away to help other people. Beyond that, he didn't ask why Dada worked in an office, what he did there, or why. He was only slightly more interested in the trucks, and on that subject he only had one question:

"Are they big trucks?"

"Yes, they're very big trucks," Dada said. In fact they were Hummers or the like.

"Oh. OK," Brandon replied, and changed the subject.

Although Brandon's phone calls with his father were mostly dull, and Brandon always seemed in a hurry to get off the phone, my phone calls with Floyd often had an edge to them: of anger or frustration, of sadness and longing, and occasionally, of fear. Despite all my rationalizations about Floyd's safety, I did have one moment when the thought of Floyd being in danger sent me into a small panic.

One day, we were talking on the phone, when I heard sirens go off, drowning out Floyd's voice. Then I picked up the faint sounds of missiles and mortar fire. "I've gotta get off the phone! I've gotta get off the phone!" Floyd yelled. "I'll call you back!" With that, the phone went dead.

I remember I was once working at a compound in Iraq when warning sirens went off. I remember how nervous I felt when I had to follow the procedures we'd drilled so many times, and find cover inside the bunkers. There was shelling uncomfortably close to our perimeter, but none of it ever hit anywhere close to where I was. In fact, nothing ever hit anywhere inside the compound at all. Still, it did make me stop and think about my mortality, and for a while after that I was much more grateful for my life every day. After a while, the euphoria wore off, and the routines kicked in, and, for the most part I didn't think about it. I just assumed that those of us who didn't go out on patrols had little to worry about.

Still, there were no guarantees, and what wife wouldn't be nervous if her soldier husband suddenly hung up the phone on the sound of wailing sirens in Afghanistan, suddenly pitching her into silence in the middle of the night in a house thousands of miles away? Heck, sometimes when

Floyd was living at home and came home late, I would worry, praying he hadn't gotten into a car wreck. Add a little artillery fire into the mix, and it could make me downright jumpy.

He didn't call for a long time.

I couldn't stand the waiting, so I tried to call back. But I couldn't get through, which, of course, made me worry more. I began pacing the kitchen, sat down in the living room and turned on the TV, stood up and sat down several times, went back to the kitchen to clean, then paced some more. "What the hell is going on over there?" Aw, forget jumpy and nervous, I'll admit, I was scared. I prayed that nothing had happened to him, would happen to him. My heart pounded as my eyes drifted to the phone and away, imagining it ringing, imagining picking it up and hearing a stranger's voice on the other end of the line, someone calling me back to tell me my husband was injured or dead—though I doubted I would get the news exactly that way.

I thanked God that Brandon was asleep. I don't know how I would have hid my panic from him.

A couple of hours later Floyd called and told me that, yes, there had been some shelling close to the perimeter, but none inside the compound. Still, it had been close enough for him to hear it, close enough for me to hear it, too close for comfort.

Sometimes it occurred to me that Brandon might be the only one in our family who was reacting rationally to our strange existence. Sometimes it seemed as if Floyd and I going on about our days as if they were routine made us adults the crazy ones. There's certainly nothing normal or routine about sending a father to war, no matter how far away the gunfire is.

* * *

It wasn't just Brandon I was trying to comfort with the idea of counting down the days until Floyd's return. I almost couldn't help counting down in my head. I was impatient for the whole nightmare with Brandon to be over, to have Floyd's help and support again, to get a frigging break. I was so excited when Brandon finally understood the idea of months, weeks, and days that it never occurred to me he might not be as interested in counting them as I was.

"Let's mark the calendar!" I said one day, as I had been saying every day since his father's return loomed, just a month away.

"I don't want to mark the calendar," Brandon said. He didn't sound angry, or sad, just… bored.

Yes, he now had some sense of how long it might be until Dada came home. But at this point he'd become so used to Dada being gone, maybe it felt easier for him not to get his hopes up by thinking about his return. As children begin to understand the passage of time, they also lose some of the joy and simplicity of living in the moment. Why should I ask Brandon to give up living that way? Waiting for "soon" hadn't exactly made my life any happier, had it? The fact was that as long as Floyd was gone, and I was carrying our life on my shoulders without a companion or lover to comfort me, I was miserable. Even though his arrival was drawing closer, I still couldn't be completely happy in the moment, and I knew I wouldn't be completely happy until my family was whole and safe again.

So we dropped the countdown idea. Or, at least we did until a couple of weeks out. Then, one late November morning, it was Brandon who brought it up. The conversation went something like this:

"Mommy, Dada is coming home in December, right?"

"That's right, baby."

"And December is after November?"

"Yes."

"How many days until December?"

"Just a few days."

"Mommy, let's mark the calendar!"

Floyd was scheduled to come home around the tenth of December. On the seventh of December, Brandon started using up lots of paper at home, to draw crayon pictures of airplanes. "Dada's coming home and he's coming home on an airplane!" he said to me, grinning from ear to ear. He understood all this because the last time Dada had come home, after my surgery, we'd picked him up from the airport. He understood because I'd pointed in the sky and told him so many times, "Dada's coming home on a plane." It had been months since I'd seen my son as happy as he was during those three days, drawing those planes.

For three days I didn't hear a peep from the school about Brandon's behavior. I don't think I realized just what a wild ball of tension my boy had become until he started to relax.

On the ninth, I received news that Floyd's plane would be arriving at oh-three-hundred hours the next day.

I explained to Brandon that this meant he would be arriving "when the clock says three-zero-zero. That's the middle of the night. So you're going to be asleep when I go pick Dada up. Do you want me to wake you up?"

"Yes," he said, nodding his head like crazy.

But he was sleeping so deeply when it was time to go, that I decided not to wake him. It didn't occur to me that I ran the risk of breaking Brandon's trust. All I was thinking was that, 1) life was about to return to normal, and 2) little boys don't always know what's best for them. Situations change, and sometimes kids just have to deal with it. Brandon was a growing boy and he needed his sleep. He would never know the difference, and by the time he did, Dada would be home.

So, I went back to that gym where so many tears had been shed the December before, and I eagerly rushed into my husband's arms for a private reunion. I didn't pull away so fast this time from all that mushy hugging and kissing.

When we came home, we both snuck into Brandon's room and sat on his bed. I placed a hand on his leg and gently rocked it, "Look who's home."

Brandon opened his eyes to see his father leaning over him. He smiled, patted Dada on the head three times, then rolled over and pretended to go back to sleep. But I knew he was just teasing. "Hey, give me a big hug!" Floyd said in a big voice. Brandon popped back up and threw his arms around him. I could feel the tears in my eyes, as I thought, *that's it, that's all he needed, just that.*

There was no fallout from my decision to let Brandon sleep when I picked up Dada. It seemed safe to trust my instincts again. There was no need to over-think these things, now that Dada was home. Brandon was, simply, thrilled to see Dada and he never called me out on breaking my promise to wake him up.

However, once he woke up, there was no getting him to go back to sleep. He stayed up until it was time to leave for school at 9:30. He just wanted to be with Dada. He almost couldn't take his eyes off the man. At first the look on his face seemed dumbfounded, as if to say, "I can't believe you're here," but it relaxed into a blissful peace the likes of which I can't ever remember seeing on his face before. His father told him about his long flight from overseas, while Brandon sat on his lap, alternately patting his arm and wrestling with him—as if to assure himself that the body he was leaning against was real. I said very little, just made breakfast and watched the two of them with a silly smile on my face. I felt the relief you feel after waking up from a nightmare and realizing that it wasn't real and everything is going to be OK.

His father walked him to the school bus, and Brandon bounced alongside him as if he might leap into the air. Both of my boys were home.

A Note to Parents:

Sometimes you need to tell yourself that the separation really will be over soon, just as much or more than you need to say it to your child. A year is a long time, but it's a finite amount of time, and if you plan enough coping strategies, and create a support system for yourself, you can get through it. I realize now that, even though I'd gotten into the habit of talking through my son's feelings with him, I wasn't processing *my* feelings with anyone. That probably would have helped both of us. And even though counting down the calendar days to Floyd's arrival was of little help to my child, it was comforting to me. Maybe I shouldn't have stopped.

My son and I were both suffering our own forms of separation anxiety. On top of that, as a parent I was also suffering from Brandon's stranglehold on my days. His problem had almost taken over my life. But living in survival mode the way I had been, I didn't really see that until it was almost too late. I didn't see it until Floyd came home, when suddenly there was someone else to be there for my child, and by extension, to be there for me.

Parents, take heed: every hour your child talks to a counselor, every hour you and your child spend making new friends, every hour you spend finding your child a school that's willing to meet more of his needs, that's one less hour that you and your child will be alone with this problem. Looking back, **I wish I'd done more to make sure that my son and I weren't each other's entire world, just because his father was gone. It was too much responsibility, and blame, for both of us to take.**

But take comfort in knowing that **children are resilient.** When

Johnny comes marching home again, as long as that return fills your home with love, that's a powerful force to have on your side as you work to help your child recover, grow, and thrive.

NINE

It Ain't Over 'Til It's Over

Although Brandon's transformation was almost like Pinocchio's, as if a fairy had magically changed him from a misbehaving wooden phony into a real boy, I could tell that it would take a long time for him to recover from our ordeal. Though he was happier, I saw signs that he didn't trust that happiness. I saw signs that his separation anxiety still lingered. It was obvious he still worried that he couldn't count on his parents to stay put and never vanish. I saw those signs on Floyd's first day home, and I still see some of those signs to this day.

The morning Floyd returned, although he took our son to the bus, I was the one who picked him up from school.

When Brandon saw me, he looked around suspiciously. "Where's Dada?" he said.

"Dada had to run an errand and will be home when we get home."

"OK," he said.

But although he seemed to take my word for it, he grew quiet and didn't play with his PlayStation on the way home the way he usually did. As the car drew closer to our house, I saw him looking out the window, craning his neck to see our house. I realized that, although he wanted to believe me, he wasn't confident his father would be there when we got home. I will say that the fact that he didn't have a meltdown when he saw me at the school without Dada shows me that he was trying to trust me. I like to think that all our talks had made that possible.

When we got home, he was ecstatic to see his father, and wore a permanent grin for the rest of the day. He spent the rest of the evening gravitating toward first Floyd and then me, never seeming to want to be alone. He was like a little sheepdog, running back and forth trying to make sure to keep his herd all in one place.

In the days and weeks that followed Floyd's return, I could tell that Brandon hadn't completely recovered from the shock of Floyd's apparent disappearance, or his fear that one of us might vanish at any time. Brandon continued to be something of a mama's boy, which wasn't something I wanted to encourage. He seemed excessively attached to me, even months later. He still followed me around the house a lot, clinging to my legs, leaning on me, sitting near me, or simply wanting to go everywhere I went.

Sometimes Floyd asked him to go to the store or to the park with him, and Brandon would ask, "Is Mama coming?" If the answer was, "No, not this time," his response was almost immediately, "Then I don't want to go."

I tried to encourage him, "Go ahead and go with Dada, honey. I'll be here when you come back." Sometimes I felt like a mama bird, pushing her chick out of the nest, as I nudged him back toward his father.

Actually, although he seemed to gravitate toward me, he seemed reluctant to leave either parent behind at the house. So even if I said, "I'm going to the store. Do you want to come?" he would hesitate.

"Is Dada coming?"

"No, sweetie."

"I'll stay with Dada."

It's as if he feared that if he left the house with one parent, the parent he left behind would pull the rug out from under him again while he was gone. I sensed that he was still insecure whenever the three of us weren't together. It's possible he was just happy to have us all together again, and eager to enjoy it. But given what he'd been through, I thought it was important to stay alert. I still do.

One thing that did change almost instantly when his father came home was that he stopped acting out at school. It was like someone simply found the switch that said "tantrums/meltdowns" and shut if off. Click: finished. Today he understands proper behavior and controls himself. I don't get calls from school or daycare anymore. Sure, sometimes the teachers say he got mad and kicked a wall, or he didn't want to sleep at naptime. But those are simple things that other kids his age might do now and then. We talk to him, we discipline him, we monitor his behavior. And mostly what we see is a boy who is starting to thrive.

I had been worried that some of the silent stubbornness and aggression he'd developed when Floyd was gone were going to become a permanent part of his personality. At one point his pre-K teacher had told me that Brandon showed signs of being gifted and might benefit from a gifted class. But, although he understood concepts past his age level, during his father's year away he mostly refused to talk in class. Whenever I came to his class, he was very talkative, eager to show off in front of me. But when I wasn't in the classroom, he turned in on himself again and fell silent. I told the teacher I didn't want to put him in an advanced class until I knew that he could be counted on to participate. He was inclined to agree.

I thought maybe that was just going to be the Brandon I would have to contend with for the rest of his school years.

But when Floyd came home, just as the tantrum switch turned off, the participation switch flipped on. It's as if Floyd brought Brandon's confidence back home with him from Afghanistan. Now Brandon interacts in class, he talks more, and he's become quite a little leader. Brandon loves to ask and answer questions, and to share what he knows with kids who need a little extra help.

Almost overnight, Brandon has changed from a withdrawn little boy to a take-charge kind of guy.

In many ways, it's as if Brandon's downward spiral during Floyd's deployment never even happened. The child that seemed demon-possessed, so that I thought he might need an exorcist—has vanished. Traces of Brandon's old separation anxieties still show up now and then: if he's in an unfamiliar situation he'll clam up, and he still seems anxious when one parent is absent from the scene at home. But I believe he'll grow into an emotionally confident young man in time.

The hell is over, the storm has past. But it may be years before we know what the long-term effects were on our son. We may never know.

* * *

Shortly after Floyd returned home, we reconsidered his military status. He had hoped to stay with the military until 2012, when he would have twenty-two years in and be entitled to full benefits and more retirement pay. But, as much as it pained us, Floyd was as convinced as I was that it wouldn't be worth it: another deployment might devastate our son and destroy our family. This decision was driven by the fact that we had been informed that if Floyd were to stay with the army, they were going to ship him to Germany, where we would have to move as a family. Going to Germany would almost certainly guarantee him another rotation to Afghanistan. I wasn't sure Brandon could handle the move to Germany after all we'd been through, and I thought he might go completely off the deep end if Floyd returned to Afghanistan.

It wasn't as if Floyd and I argued about this. He believed and understood everything that I told him about my year with Brandon. This wasn't just secondhand information from me, either; he had personally experienced Brandon's cold-shoulder treatment whenever he'd called home from overseas. Floyd knew that this problem was very real. He was as convinced as I was that he needed to make this choice for our family. We were definitely of the same mind on that. I was grateful that he was so understanding.

I know that many servicemen and –women try to put themselves in the shoes of their family struggling back home when they're overseas. But not all of them succeed in seeing the pressures as they are. It's tough for both the person deployed and those left behind, and it's an oversimplification to try to compare the two experiences.

Sure, serving in a war is dangerous, and for many soldiers it causes physical and psychological injuries they will never completely overcome. But those at home serve, too, and the psychological damage done to them can be insidious because it's so hard to see or define. Everyone at least thinks they understand the sacrifice of the soldier. But the sacrifice of the family? What exactly is it? It seems to me that if the military began looking at that question, it might save a lot of children from the kind of invisible scars that may affect Brandon for life.

What Brandon went through, he went through during a critical time of personality development. Many psychology experts believe that a child's personality is set by five, or even earlier. Brandon's personality and character have been largely shaped by the fact that his father was serving in a war for two of the most critical years of his development. And Brandon is just one of thousands.

What will the effects be on all of the children of America's active duty soldiers, children who are, in a sense, called on to serve their country before they're old enough to understand what that means?

A Note to Parents:

Don't assume that just because the storm has passed, your child is unaffected by the ordeal of long-term separation from a military parent. Small children don't understand the reasons adults do the things they do, even when the reasons are good ones. So when a father or mother leaves for a year, it feels like abandonment, regardless of whether you're serving your country, regardless of whether you want to leave or not, regardless of how often you tell the child you love them.

When the military parent returns, the only thing that will prove to a child that you both can be counted on is your concerted effort to be consistently reliable and involved… over time.

Although I'm glad Floyd chose not to continue his military service and face the possibility of another deployment, I don't think every family needs to make such a total change just because a child suffers separation anxiety disorder. Brandon's case was severe, and not every child will react so strongly. Even Brandon might not have reacted the same way again. At six years old, he might have been mature enough to begin to understand the reasons for his father's absence, he would have been old enough to have developed more coping skills, and he would have been better able to remember that he'd survived the situation before—giving him more confidence to get through it again. Still, our family is important to us, and if it wasn't absolutely necessary to take the risk, we didn't think it was worth it.

If you've made mistakes, lost your temper, or gone a little bananas around your kids during your spouse's absence, don't fear that you've done permanent damage to your child. All parents make mistakes, even under the best of circumstances. If you love your children and do your best, that can cover a multitude of errors. If you learn nothing else from my example, I hope it's this: it's never too late to learn from your mistakes and be a better parent.

I know now that if Brandon's behavior goes through a sudden, severe change in future, I won't immediately assume that he's gone to the dark side and needs more discipline to straighten him out. First, I'll ask some questions. If we cannot work it out as a family, then I'll probably take him to a counselor—and stick with it this time.

Does that mean I'll never discipline my son again? Of course not. All children need, and ultimately want, discipline to help them navigate a difficult world. If Brandon misbehaves or fails to follow the house rules in future, there will definitely be consequences. I just think it's important to be sure that when it comes time to deal out the tough consequences, that we're dealing them out to a mentally strong, emotionally healthy child, and not to a boy in crisis.

TEN

As Long as There are Wars

I loved my service in the military and my work with military contractors. I enjoyed the training and discipline, the camaraderie and friendships, the opportunities to advance in a career and to travel. Yet, after my experience as the wife of a soldier, left alone to care for a child with separation anxiety disorder, finding myself without information or support—I realized that the army I'd always admired wasn't perfect. The military offers many services for families, but it now seems to me that its service providers could use some more information on the kinds of help that families need.

I gave up two years with my husband, spent two years taking care of a household alone, and spent two years raising a child without a father, and I thought of those things as another kind of service to my country. But my child and I spent a good half of one of those years in domestic hell, directly caused by my husband's foreign deployment. And when that happened, it seemed as if our country forgot about us.

Separation anxiety is common among children who must endure extended time away from a parent. *Yet the U.S. Army didn't include the topic of "separation anxiety" in its pre-deployment briefings or materials.*

Maybe one of the military's service arms would have provided information on the topic to someone who asked for it, though I still don't know if that's true or not. Even if the information is out there, it would require parents to know that a problem exists before they could ask for information on it.

Not only did we not know about separation anxiety as a military family, but the staff of our military daycare facility didn't seem well informed on the subject either. That, even though those facilities operate under the military's auspices, and even though those facilities are filled with the children of military men and women who might face deployment at anytime. In other words, in the place most likely to see a high rate of separation anxiety in children, most of the staff was not trained to inform parents about the possibilities of separation anxiety, nor were they trained to identify and deal with separation anxiety in the children under their care. *In my son's army-run daycare center, there was just one counselor with knowledge in this area, and I never met that person until after my son's problems became severe.*

Even when I did learn about separation anxiety, months after my child was affected by it, the information available was limited. As my son's teachers and I, his school counselor and I, and then his therapist and I, all tried to figure out how to help him, I felt as if we were the blind leading the blind. Everything I did for my son during his time of crisis was reactive, nothing was pro-active. I couldn't get out ahead of this problem, because I'd received no warning.

Looking back, I believe it would have helped our family and many others if the military had asked a small panel of experts in child psychology and/or development to create a brief pamphlet on the subject of separation anxiety. *I think I might have gained a lot from just a few pages on: prevention, warning signs, what parents can do to help, when and where to seek treatment, and where parents can find support.* If someone had told us it was important to read that pamphlet, I would have read it. I served in the military; I understand the importance of following instructions. I would have informed myself, instead of remaining in the dark.

I believe it might also be helpful if the army considered providing family training sessions, to teach families practical solutions to deal with the many difficult impacts of separation during deployment. Such a session could include a family counselor or child development expert who understands separation anxiety, someone who could explain to parents what to expect. This expert could inform parents about which kinds of reactions are normal in a child and which aren't. The expert could explain what parents can do to prevent or minimize separation anxiety, how to recognize it if it strikes, what steps to take to help a child deal with it, and where to get outside help if the anxiety becomes crippling in severity—as it did in our case.

Heck, even just a single information sheet might be a start, one that says something like: "In Case Your Child Suffers From Separation Anxiety..." followed by a list of names and phone numbers for places to go and people to talk to for help. When Brandon began to have meltdowns, if I'd had a phone list of professional organizations, support groups, online resources, counselors, and the like, I would have used it until it was wrinkled and faded.

Once my son began his downward spiral, I did receive information from counselors, but the information was poorly delivered, insufficient, and inefficient. Looking back, I'm surprised that the staff at any kind of daycare center would have no clue about the warning signs of separation anxiety, much less the staff at a military daycare. If any of the childcare workers did have training in the subject, their knowledge wasn't helping us.

As for the one counselor on staff who was familiar with childhood psychology: that was a rotating position. I never even knew the daycare center had any kind of counselor until my son had been going there for several years. I believe she was only around for a few months, as were the person before her and the person after her. As far as I know, the counselor was tucked away in an office most of the time. I don't even know if that person was always on the premises.

The first day I met the counselor was when the director of the facility assigned her to observe Brandon and meet with me. As far as I know, the day she was assigned to observe my son was the first day she'd ever really met him. To me, this signaled a backwards approach. I think the military and its parents need to consider some obvious questions:

1. In a facility that is more likely to see children with emotional and behavioral issues surrounding abandonment and separation anxiety, why is the counselor the only one on staff trained in those issues?
2. Why isn't the counselor more actively involved in the daycare program on a daily basis, so that he or she can spot potential problems before they blow up?
3. Why aren't parents introduced to the counselor from the beginning, so that everyone is on the same page about watching for and preventing this potential childhood problem, which is so likely to be prevalent in a military setting?
4. Why aren't military daycare providers and military parents working together to stay informed on separation anxiety, and to create plans for dealing with it when it occurs?

The reason parents like me take their children to daycare is because we have other responsibilities to attend to and we need someone to help take care of our children while we attend to those responsibilities.

Certainly parents cannot expect a daycare center to take on a parental role whenever the child has psychological and behavioral problems that fall outside reasonable expectations. But in a military setting, the definition of reasonable expectations may need to be reconsidered. Brandon was not the only child in his daycare facility who was suffering severe and disruptive separation anxiety issues.

Out of some 12 to 15 military children in my son's class, I observed between three and five other children acting out in ways strikingly similar to Brandon. *That's up to one-third of the class.* They threw violent temper tantrums: often hitting, kicking, and biting other children or teachers. Many of them tore up the classroom: throwing toys, kicking walls, jumping on chairs, refusing to follow rules, and generally making the environment unsafe and disruptive to learning and development. That was just what I observed in *one* classroom. There were several other rooms in that daycare center. How can a daycare operate if these things are going on every day, without any expert intervention to help the teachers deal with the problem?

I saw other parents at the daycare center who had clearly dropped what they were doing to deal with their children's problems in the middle of the day. If daycare providers need to call up to one-third of parents to deal with these situations on a regular basis, consider how much productivity is lost in the civilian sector due to missed workdays by military spouses like me. Consider how much productivity and focus may be lost in the military itself, especially when both spouses are soldiers. Some parents simply cannot leave in the middle of critical work without being reprimanded or fired.

Many soldiers earn so little pay that they have to rely on social welfare programs to help them make ends meet. What happens to those families if a spouse loses a job because a child has become so disruptive and emotional distraught that he or she cannot stay in a daycare center or make it through an entire day of school?

The counselor at my son's daycare center wasn't the only expert we dealt with. She did suggest outside therapy. So I went to my primary care doctor to get a referral for a psychologist. That psychologist gave us advice that not only didn't work, but sometimes seemed to make my son's problems worse. This psychologist was trained in separation anxiety disorder, but that did not mean she was trained in dealing with separation anxiety disorder in *military children.*

In non-military children who suffer separation anxiety disorder, the issues are typically quite different. The parents are often divorced, or sometimes one or both parents are deceased. With the child of divorced parents, the child will likely see the absent parent again, so there's an opportunity to deal with the child's anxieties as a temporary problem. With the child of a deceased parent, the child will never see the absent parent again, so there's an opportunity to get the child to come to terms with the loss, to grieve, and to move on. But with a small child whose parent is deployed on a mission overseas, neither of those is the case.

The child of a deployed soldier will not see that parent in any reasonable timeframe that a pre-school age youngster can understand. The usual solutions applied to the separation anxiety suffered by children who are upset by divorce, or who are nervous about starting daycare or school, do not apply. Learning about the place where the absent parent has been deployed, putting up photos or special mementos of the absent parent, talking about the absent parent, arranging phone calls, counting down the time until the parent's return—does help some children, but for others it can be a series of fruitless exercises that only leads to more frustration.

On the other hand, the parent is not dead, and it seems cruel at best to offer the child the option of grieving for that parent and moving on, as if they're no longer part of the child's life. The fact that the parent *might* die further complicates things. No one wants to make a promise to a child that they might have to break. The promise that a parent will come home can be devastating to a child who may feel abandoned or betrayed if that promise is broken. Certainly this possibility also exists in the civilian population, but not to anywhere near the same frequency. So, while in a civilian family, promising a child a world of certainty and safety may promise more pros than cons, doing the same for a military child may not be so simple.

All that said, a psychologist trained in dealing with separation anxiety disorder as it applies to the majority population might be ill-equipped to deal with the complexities surrounding this disorder when it appears in the children of military families.

I was certainly aware before my husband was deployed overseas that it might have consequences for my family. But I had mainly considered how much more responsibility I would have to take on at home. When it came to my son's emotional reaction, I had only considered the likelihood that my son would miss his father, and that this might make him sad. I hadn't considered the possibility that he wouldn't understand or accept our explanations for his father's absence, and that he wouldn't be able to see it as anything other than abandonment.

Sure, Floyd was instructed to talk to Brandon a couple of weeks ahead of time, explaining to his son what to expect. But instructing soldiers to prepare their children by simply showing them some maps, explaining how long Daddy (or Mommy) will be gone, and saying "I love you," is the emotional equivalent of sending a soldier into battle with a bb gun. It might offer minor protection, but it's not enough if the emotional enemy sneaks up behind your child, well-armed and ready to attack.

It seems to me that we've reached a time in our country's evolving understanding of the long-term effects of military service on individuals and families, when we need to accept that families need more information, support, and training in dealing with those effects. The military makes training videos for its soldiers. Perhaps we need to consider doing the same for soldiers' spouses and children. A soldier's family serves, too, and that service is also critical to the success of U.S. missions overseas. When families don't have the tools to cope with the sacrifices they must make back home, then it can be a distraction and a drain on the soldier overseas. It can even be a disincentive for that soldier to continue his or her service.

In a volunteer army, soldiers sign up knowing they may have to make sacrifices, even the supreme sacrifice. But as soldiers witness the destructive impacts their deployment can have on families back home, they may become less willing to force their families to make the sacrifices with them. When Floyd had the option to sign up for another tour of duty, he opted out, even though he knew he would be giving up many benefits. Others may find themselves forced to make similar choices.

In educating and training military families to deal with deployment issues, effects on children should be a top consideration, because they're the ones least prepared to look out for themselves. Training families to prevent, mitigate, and treat separation anxiety disorder needs to be a high priority, if we don't want to destroy our own families in our effort to protect this nation. If we allow our country to be destroyed from within, then protecting our country from outside enemies hardly seems worth the trouble. This country is made up of families, so if the military's mission is to protect this country, then it must also protect its families.

I think the military should also encourage and create more active family support systems. My primary experience with support groups on my husband's post involved social gatherings and welcome home parties. I suppose some people who get involved with those groups engage in networking on other subjects. But it might be helpful for spouses to create a specific support group devoted to solo-parenting issues.

There is information online about military deployments and separation anxiety in children, but typically it only offers the kind of vague, feel-good advice Floyd and I received: tell the child in advance what to expect, make sure the child knows he's loved, share feelings, share maps and globes to explore your deployment destination, create a countdown ritual. None of that helped. There's also information online explaining the signs of separation anxiety, but very little information about what to do if it happens.

The ultimate answer for separation anxiety disorder seems to be counseling, and I like to think that can be helpful for many people. But when a child is coming apart at the seams, counseling can be a slow solution to a very immediate crisis. What do you do while you're waiting for the counseling to show results? Who's going to deal with the tantrums, the missed school, missed work, and the solo parent's dissolving sanity? Again, I believe parents need a support system beyond a simple pamphlet or online list of preventions and symptoms. Real humans with real solutions need to gather together, if only to give each other someone to talk to who is going through the same thing. Better yet, they may be able to share solutions with each other, from people who've been there, not just impersonal experts with little understanding of the problems particular to the military.

If the military already has support systems for people whose children have separation anxiety disorder, I wouldn't be surprised. The military is a huge organization, and sometimes it's hard for the right hand to know what the left hand is doing. So, let me add that, if there is a support system, it's important that the information be distributed. The military might create great family programs, but if no one knows about them, they don't help anyone. Furthermore, you can't merely tell people about the existence of such a program, you also have to make sure they know that this program might apply to them. Even if I'd known there was a program for such parents, I wouldn't have gone until and unless someone explained to me that separation anxiety was an issue for military children.

I don't expect the military to do it all in addressing this issue, or to do it all at once. If someone had told me even just the bare minimum on the subject of separation anxiety, it would have helped our family. I might have realized sooner that my son hadn't suddenly become a bad boy, but was truly suffering. If I'd known that, I wouldn't have increased his suffering by hitting him. It makes me want to cry just thinking about it. I wasn't trying to hurt him, but to help him learn discipline. How could I have known that he was crying out for help? He didn't know how to tell me, and no one else had bothered to explain it, until after the damage was done.

Whether the military creates pamphlets, family classes led by child development experts, videos, support groups, increased training in their daycare centers, or all of the above, I believe it will pay off in a more efficient, motivated military. In any case, I believe we owe it to the servicemen and women who protect our borders—to protect their families.

A Note to Parents:

Here's hoping the military takes steps to offer more information and support on the subject of separation anxiety for military families. But, if you've had any experience with the military, you know that it can take a long time for change to work its way through the many channels of a massive bureaucracy. So don't wait for the military to take action for you. If you have children, or are considering having children during your spouse's time, or your time, in the service, then make sure you're as informed on the subject of separation anxiety as you can be. There are many online resources and books on the subject. Here are a few that fellow military families and I have found helpful:

- Military OneSource: provides information and resources for military families
  www.militaryonesource.com

- FOCUS (Families OverComing Under Stress): family resiliency training for military families
  www.focusproject.org

- Army FRG (Family Readiness Group): helps prepare families for deployment
  www.armyfrg.org

- Army OneSource: provides information and resources for army families
  www.myarmyonesource.com

- I'm Already Home Again: Information, books, and products to help families experiencing deployment, created by military "separations specialist" Elaine Dumler
  www.imalreadyhomeagain.com

When placing your child in a daycare or school, try to find one where the staff understands the subject of separation anxiety and has a plan for dealing with children who suffer from it. If that's not possible, provide teachers and caregivers as much information on the issue, and on your child's situation, as you can. If needed, work together with the staff on a series of action steps that you, they, and the child will go through depending on escalations in the child's behavior. Stick to that plan. **Remember, a dependable routine can ease separation anxiety.**

Staying informed isn't enough. If you live near family and friends, make sure they understand what your family is dealing with, and **ask for help when you need it.** It can be helpful if you and your child spend time bonding with other family members and close friends, so that sometimes other adults who are close to your child can step in and take care of that child when you need a break. The more time your child has to get used to those special people, and to share time with those special people in your presence, the stronger the bond will be, and the less likely that your child will feel anxious when you can't be in the picture for a few hours or a day.

It may be that you're the only person your child trusts, and that his or her anxieties might be more than your family or friends are willing or able to handle. Even if you can't get away from the house, find other ways to take a break. Maybe you can stay home, but simply invite one of your friends or one of your child's friends over to visit. That way you can have some grownup time, while you're still at home offering a comforting presence for your child.

If your child's anxieties persist or grow worse, get a counselor, and don't give up on the idea if it doesn't work right away. Counseling isn't magic dust. **Just because you don't see results in a couple of weeks or a month doesn't mean the therapy isn't helping.** This isn't just about the short-term problem of getting your child to school and you to work. It's also about the consequences separation anxiety disorder can have on your child's long-term development.

Find out if your post or base has a parent support group. If it doesn't, consider creating one of your own. Reaching out to others can help. They may have ideas you haven't thought of. Even if they don't, just having the emotional support of others who understand what you're going through can be a tremendous help in reducing stress for your entire household.

As you consider the possible solutions and approaches offered to you online, or in books, or by teachers, counselors, and experts, remember that a military child is in a unique situation, and every child has a unique personality. What helps one child may not help another. **Be open to changing and shifting your solutions to suit the individual needs of your son or daughter.**

Whatever you do, don't allow your child to turn this into a war of attrition, in which he or she just has to throw a fit big enough or long enough to wear you down and bring you under his or her control. Have compassion for your child's suffering, but have compassion for yourself, too. Find babysitters you and your child trust, and get out now and then. Make friends, relax, have fun. If there's an emergency, there are phones; you can always return home if necessary.

You and your child are in this together. You both miss the family member who has been deployed far from home. If you do your best to share your love and the love of your spouse with that child, if you help that child understand that it's OK to be sad when someone you love is gone, you'll give your child a wealth of emotional strength to draw on for a lifetime. As long as you stick together, you'll come out the other side together, and your mutual love and support can make you a stronger family for it.

About the Author

Danielle Marie Batiste-Bond has been immersed in military her entire adult life. After growing up in the tiny town of New Roads, Louisiana the Army was her passport to a wide world. She spent six years in the Army at Fort Eustis, Virginia, with stints in Haiti and Kuwait. The Army taught her  teamwork and discipline. Danielle has also enjoyed working for Kellogg Brown and Root because it gave her a continued opportunity to work around the military while overseas in Kuwait, Iraq, and Dubai.

Danielle is an Army Veteran and currently works at the VA Hospital in Hampton, Virginia helping other Veterans. She lives in Newport News, Virginia with her family including six year old son Brandon whom was the motivation for her book.

About the Author